NEW DIRECTIONS FOR YOUTH DEVELOPMENT

Theory Practice Research

summer 2008

Spiritual Development

Peter L. Benson
Eugene C. Roehlkepartain
Kathryn L. Hong

issue editors

JOSSEY-BASS™
An Imprint of
WILEY

Spiritual Development
Peter L. Benson, Eugene C. Roehlkepartain, Kathryn L. Hong (eds.)
New Directions for Youth Development, No. 118, Summer 2008
Gil G. Noam, Editor-in-Chief

Microfilm copies of issues and articles are available in 16mm and 35mm, as well as microfiche in 105mm, through University Microfilms Inc., 300 North Zeeb Road, Ann Arbor, Michigan 48106-1346.

New Directions for Youth Development (ISSN 1533-8916, electronic ISSN 1537-5781) is part of The Jossey-Bass Psychology Series and is published quarterly by Wiley Subscription Services, Inc., A Wiley Company, at Jossey-Bass, 989 Market Street, San Francisco, California 94103-1741. POSTMASTER: Send address changes to New Directions for Youth Development, Jossey-Bass, 989 Market Street, San Francisco, California 94103-1741.

Subscriptions cost $85.00 for individuals and $209.00 for institutions, agencies, and libraries. Prices subject to change. Refer to the order form that appears at the back of most volumes of this journal.

Editorial correspondence should be sent to the Editor-in-Chief, Dr. Gil G. Noam, McLean Hospital, 115 Mill Street, Belmont, MA 02478.

Cover photograph by Hans F. Meier

www.josseybass.com

Contents

Issue Editors' Notes *1*
Peter L. Benson, Eugene C. Roehlkepartain, Kathryn L. Hong

Executive Summary *5*

1. Spiritual development: A missing priority in youth development *13*
Peter L. Benson, Eugene C. Roehlkepartain
This article examines how an emerging body of international research sets the stage for addressing spiritual development as an integral part of youth development, and how attending to this dimension of life could improve the well-being of adolescents while also strengthening community life and civil society.

2. Addressing spiritual development in youth development programs and practices: Opportunities and challenges *29*
Karen Pittman, Pamela Garza, Nicole Yohalem, Stephanie Artman
The authors examine whether and how youth development programs and practices address spiritual development and how these practices reflect, contradict, and extend the themes Benson and Roehlkepartain outlined in the foundational essay. They identify emerging best practices for addressing spiritual development within a program environment.

3. Spiritual development in faith communities and secular societies *45*
John A. Emmett
As societies become more pluralistic and secularized, youth workers from both faith-based and community-based settings need to take on the new roles of curator and navigation guide to assist young people with their spiritual development.

4. Putting spiritual development of young people on the map: An English perspective *59*
Maxine Green
The National Youth Agency of the United Kingdom undertook a major examination of the role of spiritual development in youth work in the United Kingdom, including extensive dialogue about how spirituality and spiritual development are defined. This article highlights the ways that the situation in the UK can contribute to a broader understanding of spirituality in youth.

Promising Practices

Issue Editors' Notes

- How do young people come to terms with issues of meaning, purpose, and identity beyond themselves?
- How do they connect with others and the world around them?
- How do they find their place in their family, community, world, and universe?
- How do they develop their deepest, most fundamental commitments?

These are, at their core, spiritual development questions. They are also critical issues in adolescent development, particularly within frameworks of positive youth development. They are the wellspring of some of the best within young people and humanity—and the source of some of the greatest atrocities in society when the answers lead young people to alienation, hatred, or violence.

Yet these are difficult, even uncomfortable, questions in both science and practice. Fewer than 2 percent of scientific publications on adolescents address spiritual development. And when they are asked about the dimensions of development they address, youth development professionals put spiritual development at the bottom of the list—below social, emotional, cognitive, and physical development.

Part of the challenge is that leaders struggle to frame the agenda in a way that is appropriate in the public arena in a pluralistic society. Too often spiritual development is presumed to be synonymous with religious development and is thus optional or even taboo. Furthermore, the rise of "faith-based initiatives" in federal funding in the United States has led to skepticism that efforts to

NEW DIRECTIONS FOR YOUTH DEVELOPMENT, NO. 118, SUMMER 2008 © WILEY PERIODICALS, INC.
Published online in Wiley InterScience (www.interscience.wiley.com) • DOI: 10.1002/yd.251

address spiritual development are masks for religious or political agendas. As a result, we lack appropriate language, frameworks, research base, or practices that enable us to examine, understand, and strengthen this dimension of life.

Despite these challenges, the past decade has seen an explosion of interest in spirituality within youth development and related fields. National and international studies and reports have suggested that spiritual development must be addressed as part of youth development. National youth-serving systems are beginning to ask how they can more effectively address these questions in a society that has become increasingly diverse and pluralistic. The growth of positive, community-based youth development provides a platform for examining these issues within the context of an overall commitment to understanding and nurturing healthy, holistic development among all young people.

Drawing on the research and field-building efforts of Search Institute's Center for Spiritual Development in Childhood and Adolescence, this volume of *New Directions for Youth Development* frames a new dialogue about the intersections between youth development and spiritual development. It draws together leading researchers and practitioners who are exploring ways to integrate spiritual development and youth development in order to strength theory, research, and practice.

After discussion of current theory and research, a promising practices section highlights emerging promising practices for addressing spiritual development in youth development programs and practices. The first article offers the thoughts of a long-time youth work practitioner on spiritual development and its place in practice, followed by a case study of engaging young people in finding their voices on the topic of their own spiritual development. Then seven brief articles explore promising practices. In some cases (such as mentoring and service-learning), the authors integrate an understanding of spiritual development into traditional youth development programs. In other cases (such as contemplation), the authors propose how these traditional spiritual practices may be appropriately integrated into youth development settings. Together, these articles illustrate the range of possible directions for attending to this dimension of life in work with young people.

The volume closes with a discussion of the important questions raised in the volume and an annotated bibliography.

Spiritual development is a critical priority for the future of youth development in order to nurture young people holistically within a global, pluralistic context. The field of youth development must engage in ongoing dialogue and learning across theory and fields of practice, beginning here.

Peter L. Benson
Eugene C. Roehlkepartain
Kathryn L. Hong
Editors

PETER L. BENSON *is president of Search Institute, Minneapolis, Minnesota, and a codirector of its Center for Spiritual Development in Childhood and Adolescence.*

EUGENE C. ROEHLKEPARTAIN *is vice president of Search Institute, Minneapolis, Minnesota, and a codirector of its Center for Spiritual Development in Childhood and Adolescence.*

KATHRYN L. HONG *is senior projects manager at Search Institute, Minneapolis, Minnesota.*

Executive Summary

Chapter One: Spiritual development: A missing priority in youth development

Peter L. Benson, Eugene C. Roehlkepartain

Addressing the spiritual development of young people has the potential to strengthen youth work and its outcomes. Spiritual development matters because it is an intrinsic part of being human and because young people themselves view it as important. This article reviews the research that points to positive impacts of spiritual development for youth and notes that in an increasingly pluralistic society, everyone needs to build skills for negotiating religious and spiritual diversity. The authors propose that spiritual development involves, in part, the dynamic interplay of three dimensions: belonging and connecting, awareness and awakening, and a way of living. Three initial challenges and opportunities are emerging: empowering youth to explore core developmental issues, motivation and focus, and multisector engagement.

Chapter Two: Addressing spiritual development in youth development programs and practices: Opportunities and challenges

Karen Pittman, Pamela Garza, Nicole Yohalem, Stephanie Artman

If strengthening children's moral and spiritual selves is the most important challenge facing youth-serving organizations in the United States today, three things are required to respond: a clear road map of where to go and how to get there, a critical mass of champions prepared to lead the way, and candid readiness assessments and strategies for individuals and organizations ready to take on this work. More clarity is needed on defining the concepts of spiritual development and spirituality, the boundaries and bridges needed between religious and secular organizations, and the activities and practices that are both effective and allowable under separation of church and state. Immediate steps to take include engaging frontline workers across sectors and identifying strategies for integrating spiritual development into youth practice.

Chapter Three: Spiritual development in faith communities and secular societies

John A. Emmett

In this article, the author writes lyrically of the struggle of young people to find meaning and hope in an increasingly secular world, and focuses his discussion on potential roles for adults "who are in serious life-shaping relationships with young people . . . to recognize and respond to the spiritual development of young people." The first role he suggests is similar to that of a museum curator: a knowledgeable adult can provide accessibility to the artifacts and practices of various cultures and spiritual traditions, help young people understand their own experience with those artifacts, and offer possible interpretations. The second role is similar to that of a navigator on a journey of exploration.

Chapter Four: Putting spiritual development of young people on the map: An English perspective

Maxine Green

Youth work in the United Kingdom is a profession requiring three years of training, and its beginnings are strongly rooted in a spiritual (often specifically Christian) context. Until the past few decades, spirituality was also integrated within the educational system. The author argues that intentionally bringing spirituality to the center of youth work is a return to the historical and philosophical roots of youth work, with its value on the whole person, including beliefs and values. Yet there are obstacles. For example, rising concerns to protect children from abuse eclipse efforts to extend young people's development. Youth workers also report a reluctance to address spiritual questions with young people either because of their own lack of knowledge or because they fear offending someone. Two areas that would benefit from further research and reflection in the field are how spirituality can be measured, and how a youth worker's own spiritual journey shapes and is shaped by her or his work with youth. Green reminds readers that lighthearted and playful but deeply meaningful approaches are common in many traditions.

Chapter Five: Perspectives on spiritual development as part of youth development

Jane Quinn

Speaking to the issue of spiritual development from her extensive experience as a youth work practitioner, the author notes several ideas she finds particularly compelling, among them that spiritual development interacts with, yet is distinct from, moral and religious development; that spiritual development is a core construct of identity formation, one of the central tasks of adolescence; and that the spiritual dimensions of youth development relate not only to work with young people but also to motivations for engaging in this work. Engaging young people in the fundamental questions of life and being human is a task that belongs in both secular and religious settings.

Chapter Six: KidSpirit *magazine: Youth in dialogue about life's big questions*

Elizabeth Dabney Hochman

The author describes founding *KidSpirit* magazine and her experiences thus far in engaging a teen editorial board. Of special note are quotations from young people themselves, including one who defines *spirituality* as "the indescribable feeling of connection with everything . . . the unlimited question and the undefined answer: The Journey."

Chapter Seven: Youth mentoring and spiritual development

Jean E. Rhodes, Christian S. Chan

Mentoring through faith-based programs could reach some of the most severely disadvantaged youth, yet efforts could be undermined if proselytizing occurs.

Chapter Eight: The spiritual nature of service-learning

Liane J. Louie-Badua, Maura Wolf

Service-learning, by its very nature, fosters young people's spiritual development, especially in experiencing a sense of interconnectedness with others and the rest of the world; opening one's heart; and expanding self-inquiry and self-knowledge.

Chapter Nine: Coming of age and awakening to spiritual consciousness through rites of passage

David G. Blumenkrantz, Kathryn L. Hong

A contemporary American form of the ancient idea of rites of passage can guide young people toward deeper meaning and strengthen their sense of identity and connection to the community.

Chapter Ten: Contemplative education and youth development

Patricia A. Jennings

Contemplative education includes practices that aim to help a person cultivate conscious awareness, especially internal self-awareness and awareness of one's connection to the world. Such practices include meditation, movement, and the contemplation of nature. Exploration is under way to determine if these practices might assist young people in their development, as they do in adulthood.

Chapter Eleven: Spiritual development and camp experiences

Karla A. Henderson, M. Deborah Bialeschki

Camps have long addressed multiple components of young people's development, including spiritual development. In particular, transcendental communion with nature and the outdoors may provide one pathway for young people's spiritual development.

Chapter Twelve: Spiritual development in youth worker preparation: A matter of resolve

Elisabeth M. Kimball

Once we are convinced that attentiveness to spiritual development has the potential to enrich and improve youth work practice, equipping youth workers with the necessary skills and capacities can proceed. A model for such preparation begins with youth workers' reflecting on their own spiritual autobiographies.

Chapter Thirteen: Spiritual development with marginalized youth: A status report

Melanie Wilson, Kristal S. Nicholson

Efforts to clarify the appropriate uses of spirituality programming with marginalized youth are under way. Some researchers suggest that such programs should consider spiritual exploration and growth as a core part of treatment, involve youth voluntarily and as decision makers, and align programming with youth's cultural experiences.

Chapter Fourteen: Spiritual development in adolescence: Toward enriching theories, research, and professional practice

Anne C. Petersen

The author notes that she finds the case for making spiritual development a priority surprisingly compelling—"surprisingly" because although she is an expert on adolescent development, she has not done research or previously written about spiritual development. She suggests that a systems analysis occur first, before engaging frontline youth workers in this realm, to identify the interests of key stakeholder groups and ways to unleash creativity and engagement in each of them. The key will be framing engagement of spiritual development in ways that include rather than divide sectors and groups.

Resources: Spiritual development—youth development

Compiled by Sandra P. Longfellow

An annotated bibliography of this developmental intersection.

Although spiritual development has been on the margins of youth development research, policy, and practice, it deserves to be an integral focus for the field.

1

Spiritual development: A missing priority in youth development

Peter L. Benson, Eugene C. Roehlkepartain

SPIRITUAL. . . . Just saying the word can evoke strong reactions. For some, it connects with a deep reality, commitment, and set of practices that are grounded in thousands of years of tradition and divine revelation. For others, it evokes something new and creative—a corrective to the stodginess and rigidity of religion as they see it. To still others, it is a trendy catchphrase with little substance. Yet a growing number of youth leaders are recognizing an opportunity for a new (or renewed) dialogue on the place of spiritual development in youth development.

Given the term's complexity, it may be tempting to set it aside and focus on related issues of character or moral development. However, struggling to more fully integrate this domain into youth development theory, policy, and practice has significant potential to strengthen youth work and its outcomes. Furthermore, by not addressing spiritual development, we risk thwarting healthy growth in this domain or, in some cases, allowing it to become destructive.

WILEY InterScience® DISCOVER SOMETHING GREAT

Published online in Wiley InterScience (www.interscience.wiley.com) • DOI: 10.1002/yd.253

Why it matters

Why should youth development professionals be intentional in addressing spiritual development? We offer several starting points.

An integral part of being human

A growing theoretical and research literature suggests that spiritual development is an intrinsic part of being human.[1] From this perspective, spiritual development "happens" to all persons, whether secular humanists, atheists, Muslims, or Methodists. Sometimes it happens intentionally and thoughtfully. Other times it is not conscious but fully embedded in its culture.[2] Still other times, it may be destructive, leading people to harm themselves or others.[3] If part of being human is being spiritual, then a commitment to holistic development demands that we come to terms with this dimension of life. The question is, How might we integrate it into youth work while also respecting each young person's and family's worldviews, beliefs, and traditions?

Perceived importance among young people

Most young people view spiritual development as an important part of their lives. Until recently, the primary data available have focused on religious participation and importance. However, UCLA's Higher Education Research Institute recently released major research on the spiritual lives and interests of 112,232 freshmen from a national sample of 236 colleges and universities. Three-fourths (77 percent) of the students say they believe "we are all spiritual beings." The researchers highlighted other key findings as follows:

> Today's entering college students report high levels of spiritual interest and involvement. Four in five indicate "having an interest in spirituality" and "believing in the sacredness of life," and nearly two-thirds say that "my spirituality is a source of joy." Nearly half report that they consider it "essential" or "very important" to seek opportunities to help them grow spiritually.[4]

Spiritual development may be even more salient for vulnerable youth. The New England Network for Child, Youth, and Family Services conducted focus groups with 149 youth in institutional care settings. They found that 86 percent of these youth considered themselves spiritual or somewhat spiritual.[5]

Spirituality is evident early in life and throughout childhood.[6] It continues to change and be transformed throughout life through a dynamic developmental process that may involve ongoing transactions between persons and society,[7] ongoing growth in knowledge or skill,[8] or movement toward perfection.[9] However, most agree that adolescence, with its focus on identity and belonging, is a particularly formative time in a person's spiritual trajectory.

Impact on young people's well-being

Research points to the impact of spiritual development (and related concepts) in young people's lives. The current research tends to emphasize spirituality through the lens of religion and focus on adolescents who are part of mainstream religious traditions (especially Christian) in the United States. But even with these important limitations, the research base makes a compelling case.

The most comprehensive synthesis of the research is compiled in *The Handbook of Spiritual Development in Childhood and Adolescence*, which includes chapters that examine links between spiritual development and moral development, civic development, identify formation, coping, resilience, delinquency, well-being and thriving, and physical health.[10]

Similarly, Johnson reviewed more than five hundred academic articles on the impact of "organic religion" on people's lives (primarily adults). He describes organic religion as that religion which is "practiced over time, such as with children who were raised and nurtured in religious homes," thus differentiating it from institutional religion. He examines research that documents various components of organic religion as protecting against health risks such as depression, suicide, promiscuous sexual behaviors, alcohol and other drug use, and delinquency. Johnson also reviews studies showing organic religion's association with a variety of prosocial factors, such as longevity, civic engagement, well-being, and educational attainment.[11]

Although the preponderance of research points to the potential positive impact of spiritual development, there is also evidence of a side to spirituality filled with doubts, struggles, and the existential dark night of the soul, as well as, in some cases, destruction or harm to self or others.[12] This may be manifested in attitudes of intolerance toward others, delusions of grandeur, manipulation and authoritarianism, or acts of violence. These paths, though by no means normative, point to some of the value- and culturally laden challenges that may surface in seeking to examine spirituality. Although these manifestations are rare, they generate considerable attention in the media when they occur—and too few youth workers are equipped to respond constructively.

Potential for impact

The field of youth development needs to explore how to integrate spiritual development into its policies, programs, and practices because its organizations, whether secular or religious, have potential to have a positive impact on young people.

The best evidence to date may be the American Camp Association's first large-scale study of the impact of camping on youth development outcomes. This study of more than two hundred camps found statistically significant increases in spirituality from before camp began to after camp was finished. The impact was evident in both faith-based and secular camps, although the measurement items focused on religiously oriented elements of spirituality.[13]

Future research will likely yield additional insight into the potential positive impact of effective youth development practices in nurturing spiritual development. However, we must begin articulating specific contexts, practices, and experiences that intentionally cultivate spiritual development. These may include mindfulness, meditation, or prayer practices, serving others and reflecting on this "spirituality in action," deepening interconnectedness through mentoring relationships, and many others (see the articles in the Promising Practices section in this volume). Evidence from Larson, Hansen, and Moneta suggests that a programmatic emphasis on spiritual development has a particularly strong relationship with identity formation during adolescence.[14]

Attending to the mystery and intangible

The final rationale deals with the less definable dimensions of spiritual development. Green notes that youth work has been pressed to target its efforts, show public health and educational outcomes, and adopt policies and procedures that can "professionalize" the field. While acknowledging the value, she worries that increased targeting "can have a detrimental effect on the holistic, relationship-based approach which is embedded in the values of the profession. . . . Where a lot of work with young people is geared to education, employment and training, spiritual development is primarily about being a full human being."[15]

Building skills to negotiate pluralism in society

Addressing spiritual development in the curriculum of youth development touches on a related societal issue: learning to live in a religiously and spiritually pluralistic society. As Muslim activist Eboo Patel puts it, "We need a language that allows us to emphasize our unique inspirations and affirm our universal values. We need spaces where we can each state that we are proud of where we came from and all point to the place we are going to."[16] By providing a venue for these discussions that is not tied to a specific religious tradition, youth development programs address an urgent need to equip young people with the skills and perspectives to negotiate spiritual issues with mutual respect and healthy curiosity.

Coming to a shared understanding

In order to consider spiritual development a greater priority in youth development, we must come to a clearer understanding of what we mean by it. The challenge, of course, is that spirituality and spiritual development are intrinsically difficult to define. Indeed, philosophers, theologians, and other scholars have debated the nuances of this realm of life for thousands of years, and thousands of pages have been written to seek to give words and meaning to this dimension of human experience, thought, belief, and action.

The place of religion in the dialogue

Although the world's religious traditions have deep wells of wisdom to offer regarding the spiritual nurture of children and adolescents, they are often unexamined. Yust, Johnson, Sasso, and Roehlkepartain write:

> This insight [about children's spiritual nurture]—rooted in diverse cultures, worldviews, belief systems, and experiences—has often been taken for granted or assumed within the traditions. Traditions have been passed from one generation to the next, with relatively little theological or philosophical reflection on the "why" behind the beliefs and practices. Furthermore, the traditions have rarely been in dialogue with each other about young people and their spiritual nurture.[17]

Although we acknowledge the rich philosophical and religious traditions that inform our understanding, some of the resistance to exploring spiritual development lies precisely in its relation to religion. On one side is a press to separate the two ideas; on the other, they are seen as essentially the same thing.[18]

As one alternative, we propose framing spiritual development as a core developmental process that occurs for all persons, regardless of their religious beliefs. From this perspective, religious beliefs and practices can be an integral part of spiritual development, but they do not have to be. To guide and support them in this process, many people tap the belief systems, narratives, and community of a religious or cultural tradition. Other people choose other resources and contexts, including arts, philosophy, and nature.

Challenges to addressing the domain

Search Institute's work in this field seeks to draw insight from many disciplines, but the social science literature, particularly psychology, has played an important role in shaping our understanding of adolescence and youth work and education (both secular and religious).

Among the challenges in addressing spiritual development (and its cousin religion) in the social sciences is the personal rejection of religion by many social scientists and the corollary that religion, like music or politics, is a discretionary human activity.[19] Jones argues that psychology's refusal to take religion (and, by extension, spirituality) seriously is due to a prevailing but outdated philosophy of science grounded in positivism,[20] in which science is seen as trading in facts and religion as trading in faith.[21]

The exploration is also hampered by the lack of a strong theoretical base and measures consistent with that theory. Nearly every review of the literature notes the lack of a robust theory about spiritual development grounded in current understandings of human development.[22] For example, much of the literature presumes stage theories of development, now supplanted in the broader human development literature by more interactive and ecological understandings.

Numerous instruments are available to measure spiritual development.[23] However, most are grounded in theistic, North American assumptions and worldviews that emphasize religious beliefs, experiences, and practices. Several measures of spirituality are available, but they tend to focus on spiritual experiences (awe, wonder) without a broader developmental and ecological context. Furthermore, most have not been validated with young people, and the research using these scales tends to be cross-sectional and with small samples.[24]

Recent years have seen many efforts to define spirituality and its relationship with religion. Some of these tie spirituality to the concept of the sacred,[25] while others focus on spirituality as a set of human qualities (such as insight and understanding, a posture of generosity and gratitude) without explicit reference to a sacred or transcendent realm.[26]

Explicating assumptions

By seeking to clarify our own working definitions and assumptions, we will be better able to engage in dialogue and learning with others who may or may not share those assumptions. We have chosen to understand spiritual development as a set of core developmental processes that have not been fully articulated by other streams of development (for example, cognitive, social, emotional, moral, and physical). In 2003, we first offered this working definition:

Spiritual development is the process of growing the intrinsic human capacity for self-transcendence, in which the self is embedded in something greater than the self, including the sacred. It is the developmental "engine" that propels the search for connectedness, meaning, purpose and contribution. It is shaped both within and outside of religious traditions, beliefs and practices.[27]

However, this working definition was only a starting point. To broaden the conversation, we engaged 120 scientific, theological, and practice advisers from around the world in a Web-based consensus-building process around spiritual development.[28] Advisers critiqued and recommended criteria, ranked various dimensions of spiritual development, and offered other guidance as we sought to create a framework for understanding child and adolescent spiritual development as an integral part of human development.

An emerging consensus-based framework

What is emerging is a sense that "spirit" may be an intrinsic capacity or part of life that propels young people to embed themselves in something larger than themselves. It speaks to what it means to be human—what William James called "the primordial thing," out of which grow art, philosophy, and theology.[29] Indeed, the word *spirit* comes from the Latin *spiritus*, meaning breath expressed with vigor and courage.[30]

Spiritual development, then, is an ongoing, dynamic, and sometimes difficult interplay between one's inward journey and one's outward journey. It presses us to look inward to accept or discover our potential to grow, contribute, and matter, and to look outward to connect with life, including being in relationship with family, community, the world, and, for many, the sacred, divine, or some form of universal reality.

Through a series of feedback loops with advisers, a broad (though not unanimous) consensus has emerged that spiritual development may involve the dynamic interplay of at least three processes:

- *Awareness or awakening.* Being or becoming aware of or awakening to one's self, others, and the universe (which may be understood as including the sacred or divinity) in ways that cultivate identity, meaning, and purpose.
- *Interconnecting and belonging.* Seeking, accepting, or experiencing significance in relationships to and interdependence with others, the world, or one's sense of the transcendent (often including an understanding of God or a higher power); and linking to narratives, beliefs, and traditions that give meaning to human experience across time.
- *A way of living.* Authentically expressing one's identity, passions, values, and creativity through relationships, activities, and practices that shape bonds with oneself, family, community, humanity, the world, and that which one believes to be transcendent or sacred.

Each of these processes (which we are just beginning to explicate) is multilayered and dynamic, at work across cultures and across the age span in many different ways. Sometimes these dynamics are grounded in an understanding or experience of transcendence, including an understanding of God, a higher power, or other transcendent forces.

Consistent with current developmental theories, our use of the term *development* emphasizes change across time. It does not imply a linear, invariant progression of universal stages; rather, it suggests a set of core processes that vary in how they occur. This approach is consistent with Sroufe's view of development as a "succession of branchings" that enable individuals on different pathways to nevertheless "converge toward similar patterns of adaptation."[31]

These three processes are not the full picture, as suggested in Figure 1.1. They are embedded in and interact with (d) other aspects of development (for example, physical, social, cognitive, emotional, moral); (e) personal, family, and community beliefs, values, and practices; (f) culture (language, customs, norms, symbols) and sociopolitical realities; (g) meta-narratives, traditions, myths, and interpretive frameworks; and (h) other significant life events, experiences, and changes. These processes may result in

Figure 1.1. Conceptual model of components of spiritual development

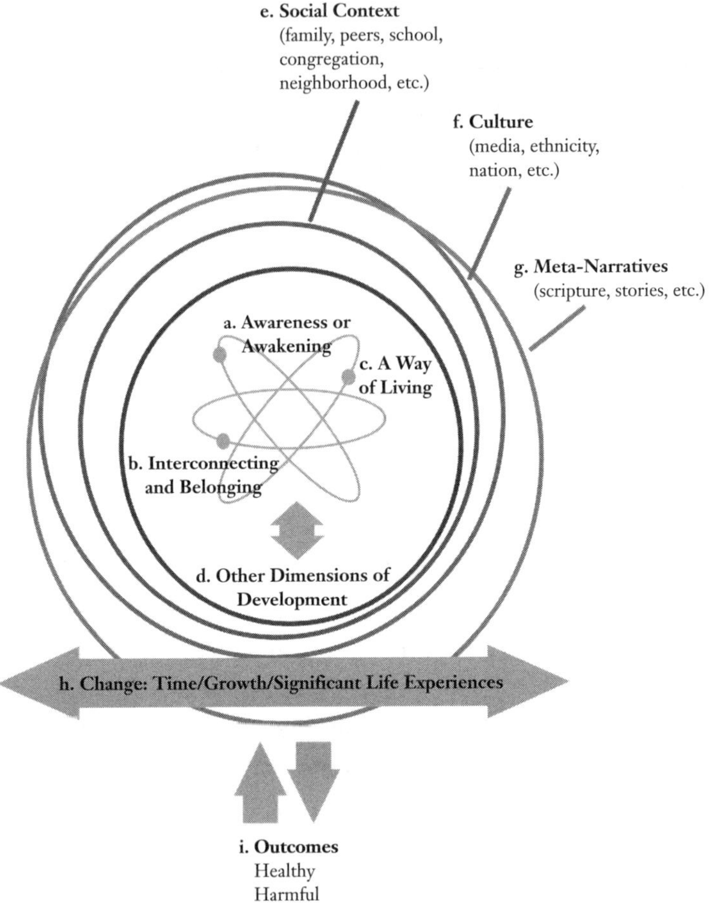

(i) cognitive, affective, physical, and social outcomes that become manifested in healthy or unhealthy ways.

Less clear from a theoretical and empirical perspective is how this dimension of life interacts with other domains of development. Research suggests that spiritual development interacts with many other dimensions of development: cognitive, emotional, moral, personality, and physical.[32] Scholars debate whether it is a subset of other domains (like cognitive development) or whether it is distinct though linked. Others suggest that spiritual development may be an integrating domain of development that helps to weave the others together. However, until the field has a solid theoretical foundation that can be empirically tested, it is impossible to reach definitive conclusions.

Our working framework attempts to shed light on these issues. At the time of this writing, we are developing a survey to test this framework in an exploratory study on multiple continents. Those findings will give new insight into how the processes work in young people's lives and set the stage for more rigorous research, including longitudinal research. In addition, we intend to develop tools and guides to use the framework (as it evolves) in dialogue and work with young people. Once we have evidence of its reliability and validity, it may serve as a framework for infusing spiritual development themes into youth development programs and practices—and, potentially, as the foundation for more robust studies that examine programmatic impact.

Opportunities and challenges

Gaining some level of consensus on the definition and dimensions is the first step, and it has only begun. The youth development field must also work through several challenges and opportunities before it can embrace spiritual development as an essential priority for youth development.

Empowering youth to explore core developmental issues

In conducting focus groups, we found that young people often do not have language and frames to explore this dimension of life. However, as the conversation progressed and they became more comfortable, most wished they had more opportunities to engage in similar dialogues. Yet addressing spiritual issues in youth development settings must be done with care. Youth workers must be equipped to help youth negotiate the questions in healthy, empowering, and respectful ways. If not, they may revert to their own (sometimes narrow) religious perspective as the only frame they know. If they become intentional and competent regarding spiritual development within a pluralistic society, they can be adept at helping young people explore core questions in fresh, engaging ways.

Multisector engagement

A key insight in positive youth development is that all socializing systems affect all aspects of young people's development.[33] Single institutions do not have exclusive responsibility for specific parts of young people's development. If diverse youth development organizations seek to become more intentional in spiritual development and if faith-based organizations recognize the roles of others in this domain, it may open a dialogue across sectors that reinvigorates commitments to holistic development in both.[34]

At the same time, we must be candid about why we do this vital work. Are we doing it because we recognize that it is part of human development that merits greater attentiveness? If instead it is motivated by an exclusivistic religious agenda that seeks to impose religious beliefs on public, pluralistic, or secular contexts, legitimate questions can—and should—be raised.

Church and state issues

What is the place of spiritual development in a secular or pluralistic society? Do public (governments, schools), community-based, and other private institutions have any role to play? Specific answers to these questions will vary by country and context. To the extent that we view spiritual development as integral to human development, then broad engagement would likely be possible and constructive. If, however, the approach taken to spiritual development is de facto grounded in a majority religious tradition (such as Christianity in the United Kingdom or the United States or Islam in Iran or Malaysia), then concern among minority religious groups as well as citizens who are secular in their outlook is legitimate.

On a practical level, this distinction requires that youth workers, educators, and others develop skills, competencies, and practices that support young people in their spiritual development without imposing (even subtly) their own worldview. Perhaps infusing the training, attitudes, and practices that have been refined in multicultural education into approaches to spiritual development can create the safe, respectful environments in which young people can explore and cultivate their own spiritual identities.

Exploring diverse approaches

If spiritual development is integral to human development across the life span, how will our practice be different? We would suggest that the U.S. default of programmatic, didactic models of education is inadequate, even counterproductive. Alternate approaches include, for example, the work of Maria Montessori, whose view of children as self-directed learners led her to design learning environments and experiences based less on imposed content and more on observing and listening to children, then encouraging them to take a lead in guiding their own growth and learning.[35] This and the articles in the Promising Practices section of this volume begin to suggest the range of approaches that may be available as the field of youth development more fully integrates spiritual development.

Framing an overdue conversation

With this volume of *New Directions for Youth Development*, we seek to advance a conversation in the field about whether and how spiritual development might become a priority, allowing us to truly address young people's development holistically.

We have begun by asking the contributors to this volume to reflect on and respond to the issues and frameworks we offer, while extending the conversation in other important new directions as well. We hope that through respectful, thoughtful dialogue, we can find a space for advancing the field and, in the process, more effectively nurturing and learning from the young people in our care and in our midst.

Notes

1. Benson, P. L., Roehlkepartain, E. C., & Rude, S. P. (2003). Spiritual development in childhood and adolescence: Toward a field of inquiry. *Applied Developmental Science,* 7(3), 204–212; Oser, F. K., Scarlett, W. G., & Bucher, A. (2006). Religious and spiritual development throughout the life span. In W. Damon & R. M. Lerner (Eds.), *Handbook of child psychology, Vol. 1: Theoretical models of human development* (6th ed., pp. 942–998). Hoboken, NJ: Wiley; Roehlkepartain, E. C., King, P. E., Wagener, L. M., & Benson, P. L. (Eds.). (2006). *The handbook of spiritual development in childhood and adolescence.* Thousand Oaks, CA: Sage.
2. Gottlieb, A. (2006). Non-Western approaches to spiritual development among infants and young children: A case study from West Africa. In E. C. Roehlkepartain, P. E. King, L. M. Wagener, & P. L. Benson (Eds.), *The handbook of spiritual development in childhood and adolescence* (pp. 60–72). Thousand Oaks, CA: Sage.
3. Wagener, L. M., & Mahoney, H. N. (2006). Spiritual and religious pathology in adolescence. In E. C. Roehlkepartain, P. E. King, L. M. Wagener, & P. L. Benson (Eds.), *The handbook of spiritual development in childhood and adolescence* (pp. 137–149). Thousand Oaks, CA: Sage.
4. Astin, A. W., Astin, H. S., Lindholm, J. A., Bryant, A. N., Szelényi, K., & Calderone, S. (2005). *The spiritual life of college students: A national study of college students' search for meaning and purpose.* Los Angeles: Higher Education Research Institute, UCLA. Also see Smith, C., with Denton, M. L. (2005). *Soul searching: The religious and spiritual lives of American teenagers.* New York: Oxford University Press.
5. Wilson, M. (2004). *A part of you so deep: What vulnerable adolescents have to say about spirituality.* Boxborough, MA: New England Network for Child, Youth and Family Services.
6. Hay, D., & Nye, R. (1998). *The spirit of the child.* London: Fount/HarperCollins; Rosengren, K. S., Johnson, C. N., & Harris, P. L. (Eds.). (2000). *Imagining the impossible: Magical, scientific, and religious thinking in children.* Cambridge: Cambridge University Press.
7. Lerner, R. M., Albert, A. E., Anderson, P. M., & Dowling, E. M. (2006). On making humans human: Spirituality and the promotion of positive youth development. In E. C. Roehlkepartain, P. E. King, L. M. Wagener, & P. L. Benson (Eds.), *The handbook of spiritual development in childhood and adolescence* (pp. 150–162). Thousand Oaks, CA: Sage.
8. Feldman, D. H. (1985). *Beyond universals in cognitive development.* Norwood, NJ: Ablex.
9. Kaplan, B. (1983). Genetic-dramatism: Old wine in new bottles. In B. Kaplan (Ed.), *Toward a holistic developmental psychology* (pp. 53–75). Mahwah, NJ: Erlbaum.
10. Roehlkepartain et al. (2006).

11. Johnson, B. R. (2008). A tale of two religious effects: Evidence for the protective and prosocial impact of organic religion. In K. K. Kline (Ed.), *Authoritative communities: The scientific case for nurturing the whole child* (pp. 187–226). New York: Springer.

12. Atran, S. (2002). *In gods we trust: The evolutionary landscape of religion.* Oxford: Oxford University Press; Wagener and Mahoney. (2006).

13. American Camp Association. (2005). *Directions: Youth development outcomes of the camp experience.* Martinsville, IN: Author.

14. Larson, R. W., Hansen, D. M., & Moneta, G. (2006). Differing profiles of developmental experiences across types of organized youth activities. *Developmental Psychology, 42*(5), 849–863.

15. Green, M. (2005). *Spirituality and spiritual development in youth work: A consultation paper from the National Youth Agency.* Leicester, UK: National Youth Agency. Retrieved June 1, 2007, from www.nya.org.uk.

16. Patel, E. (2007). *Acts of faith: The story of an American Muslim: The struggle for the soul of a generation.* Boston: Beacon Press.

17. Yust, K. M., Johnson, A. N., Sasso, S. E., & Roehlkepartain, E. C. (Eds.). (2006). *Nurturing child and adolescent spirituality: Perspectives from the world's religious traditions.* Lanham, MD: Rowman and Littlefield.

18. Hill, P. C., Pargament, K. I., Hood, R. W., McCullough, M. E., Swyers, J. P., Larson, D. B. et al. (2000). Conceptualizing religion and spirituality: Points of commonality, points of departure. *Journal for the Theory of Social Behavior, 30*(1), 52–77.

19. Wulff, D. M. (1997). *Psychology of religion: Classic and contemporary.* Hoboken, NJ: Wiley.

20. Jones, S. L. (1994). A constructive relationship for religion with the science and profession of psychology: Perhaps the boldest model yet. *American Psychologist, 49*(3), 184–199.

21. Benson, P. L. (2006). The science of child and adolescent spiritual development: Definitional, theoretical, and field-building challenges. In E. C. Roehlkepartain, P. E. King, L. M. Wagener, & P. L. Benson (Eds.), *The handbook of spiritual development in childhood and adolescence* (pp. 484–499). Thousand Oaks, CA: Sage.

22. Oser et al. (2006).

23. Compiled at www.spiritualdevelopmentcenter.org/measure; also see Hill, P. C., & Hood, R. W. (1999). *Measures of religiosity.* Birmingham, AL: Religious Education Press; Tsang, J. A., & McCullough, M. E. (2003). Measuring religious constructs: A hierarchical approach to construct organization and scale selection. In S. J. Lopez & C. R. Snyder (Eds.), *Positive psychological assessments: A handbook of models and measures* (pp. 345–360). Washington, DC: American Psychological Association.

24. Benson. (2006).

25. Hill et al. (2000); Miller, W. R., & Thoresen, C. E. (2003). Spirituality, religion, and health. *American Psychologist, 58*(1), 24–35; Pargament, K. I. (1999). The psychology of religion and spirituality? Yes and no. *International Journal for the Psychology of Religion, 9*(1), 3–16.

26. Beck, U. (1992). *Risk society: Towards a new modernity.* Thousand Oaks, CA: Sage; Roof, W. C. (1993). *A generation of seekers: The spiritual journeys of the baby boom generation.* San Francisco: HarperCollins.

27. Benson et al. (2003).

28. See the listing at www.spiritualdevelopmentcenter.org/Advisors.

29. James, W. (1902). *The varieties of religious experience: A study in human nature.* New York: Modern Library.

30. Benson, P. L. (2007, June). Spiritual development and adolescence. *Family Focus* (National Council on Family Relations), pp. 3, 19.

31. Sroufe, A. L. (1997). Psychopathology as an outcome of development. *Development and Psychopathology, 9,* 251–268.

32. Roehlkepartain et al. (2006).

33. Benson, P. L., Scales, P. C., Hamilton, S. F., and Sesma, A. (2006). Positive youth development: Theory, research, and applications. In W. Damon & R. M. Lerner (Eds.), *Handbook of child psychology, Vol. 1: Theoretical models of human development* (6th ed., pp. 894–941). Hoboken, NJ: Wiley.

34. Garza, P., Artman, S., Roehlkepartain, E. C. (2007). *Is there common ground? An exploratory study of the interests and needs of community-based and faith-based youth workers.* Washington, DC: National Collaboration for Youth and Minneapolis: Search Institute.

35. Montessori, M. (1973). *From Childhood to Adolescence.* New York: Schocken.

PETER L. BENSON *is president of Search Institute, Minneapolis, Minnesota, and a codirector of its Center for Spiritual Development in Childhood and Adolescence.*

EUGENE C. ROEHLKEPARTAIN *is vice president of Search Institute, Minneapolis, Minnesota, and a codirector of its Center for Spiritual Development in Childhood and Adolescence.*

Youth workers and youth programs are poised to make spiritual development a more explicit part of their offerings if they can get a clearer road map for navigating this territory.

2

Addressing spiritual development in youth development programs and practices: Opportunities and challenges

Karen Pittman, Pamela Garza, Nicole Yohalem, Stephanie Artman

> In a society in which pluralism is a fact and freedom a birthright, finding new ways to strengthen and not ignore or stunt children's moral and spiritual selves may be the single most important challenge facing youth professionals and youth-serving organizations in the U.S. today.
>
> Commission on Children at Risk,
> *Hardwired to Connect* (2003)

THOSE WHO WORK WITH youth in voluntary, structured but informal programs and settings frequently grapple with whether, when, where, and how to assist young people in their spiritual development. They rarely, however, question why.

Published online in Wiley InterScience (www.interscience.wiley.com) • DOI: 10.1002/yd.254

Youth development professionals and organizations are usually associated with their efforts to address young people's social, physical or civic development. The activities and places associated with these goals—clubs, camps, troops, teams, after-school centers, and community service projects—are the most common and most visible. But youth workers have always considered spiritual or moral development to be an essential part of their work, no matter what their presenting activities are.

Breaking the silence

Why, then, are youth workers and, even more important, the directors and boards of youth-serving organizations relatively silent on this topic? Why is spiritual development not advertised as a key program outcome or practice? If the assertion of the Commission on Children at Risk in *Hardwired to Connect* is correct, what will it take to respond to the "most important challenge facing youth professionals and youth-serving organizations in the U.S. today"?[1]

We believe it will take three things: a clear road map of where to go and how to get there, a critical mass of professionals prepared to lead the way, and candid assessments to identify the individuals and organizations ready to take on this work and strategies for helping them succeed.

Goal 1: A clear road map

A review of recent research studies and youth worker surveys, combined with field knowledge and opportunistic field interviews, produced four reasons that youth development programs and professionals may be less than transparent about their commitment to youth's spiritual development:

The concepts are not clear. *Religion* and *spirituality* are powerful words linked to powerful but unclear concepts that define cultures and shape values. They are also powerful words that are used almost interchangeably. The distinction is unclear. Hay, Reich, and Utsch define religious development as "the process through which a person's basic selection of parts of an institutionalized religion, together with his or her own religious ideas and concepts, becomes a mature religiosity."[2]

Benson and Roehlkepartain review the origins and status of the debates over the distinction between religious and spiritual development in the opening article of this volume. We appreciate their efforts and, more important, their offer in 2003 of a three-part definition of spirituality as a core developmental process ("the process of growing the intrinsic human capacity for self-transcendence"), an engine ("the engine that propels the search for connectedness, meaning, purpose and contribution"), and a product of contexts ("shaped both within and outside of religious traditions, practices and beliefs"). Now in 2008, their definition has evolved to include the idea that

> spiritual development may involve the dynamic interplay of at least three developmental processes:
>
> - *Awareness or awakening.* Being or becoming aware of or awakening to one's self, others, and the universe (which may be understood as including the sacred or divinity) in ways that cultivate identity, meaning, and purpose.
> - *Interconnecting and belonging.* Seeking, accepting, or experiencing significance in relationships to and interdependence with others, the world, or one's sense of the transcendent (often including an understanding of God or a higher power); and linking to narratives, beliefs, and traditions that give meaning to human experience across time.
> - *A way of living.* Authentically expressing one's identity, passions, values, and creativity through relationships, activities, and practices that shape bonds with oneself, family, community, humanity, the world, and that which one believes to be transcendent or sacred.

This type of formulation, while complex, resonates with youth workers who understand that development—cognitive, civic, social, physical, and spiritual—is a complex growth process that is linked to definable outcomes and influenced by the multiple environments that young people traverse.[3]

Templeton and Eccles's definition gets to the point of the confusion even more quickly. They define spiritual identity as "a personal identity" consisting of "spiritual characteristics unique to the individual rather than shared with a group." They suggest that spiritual identity "is not associated directly with feelings of belonging to a religious group."[4]

Perhaps most comforting to professionals, parents, and perhaps faith leaders is that the distinction between spirituality and religiosity seems to be clear to young people. Wilson conducted focus groups, interviews, and surveys of adolescents in researching her book *A Part of You So Deep.* Her findings: "90 percent of youth said that a person could be spiritual without being religious—a finding consistent with research showing that while interest in organized religion may dwindle during adolescence, interest in spirituality itself does not." Spirituality for these young people was more about finding and maintaining an inner compass than holding a set of shared beliefs.[5]

The scope of authority is not clear. Spirituality may be a universal need that transcends specific religions, but as long as it is closely associated with religion, secular organizations and institutions will be reluctant to take formal responsibility for supporting spiritual development. Hence, staff and youth may perceive the need to address it informally in ways that go unnoticed or undocumented by directors.

As Benson and Roehlkepartain note, community-based youth workers and youth-serving organizations acknowledged the need to support spiritual development more than they reported doing so. In *Is There Common Ground?* the authors found that only 14 percent of community-based workers (compared to 77 percent of faith-based workers) believed that "helping young people develop spiritually" was an essential part of their work. This 2007 report summarizes the findings from two Web-based surveys of youth workers from both secular and faith-based organizations. The surveys were done as part of an exploration of the possibility of the two groups learning from each other and sharing training in core competencies. Yet almost four out of ten of both community- and faith-based workers thought that it was important to help young people respect and honor religious diversity.[6]

In *Practice Unbound,* Melanie Wilson reports that the most common reason youth-serving agencies offered for not providing secular spiritual activities was the conservatism of board members, executive-level staff, or direct service staff. (See also the article by

Elisabeth M. Kimball in this volume.) One of the agency executives interviewed commented that both the community and agency held such traditional views that "such activities" would never fly, unless, perhaps, the agency had an outside expert come in "on a piecemeal basis."[7]

This conservatism may be related to a desire to limit business liabilities. The "church-state thing," as one youth worker called it, is a real or perceived barrier for staff and boards who are unsure what the rules are.[8] Steering clear of gray areas is often a wise course. This conservatism could also reflect the belief that religious instruction is best handled by families and faith institutions or that, again, it is prudent to steer clear of these topics when working with youth from different or unknown backgrounds.

In either case, clear distinctions between spirituality and religion might help, especially if these distinctions were not only shared but jointly proclaimed by both religious and secular groups such as the Interfaith Youth Core and the National Collaboration for Youth. By combining forces across faith-based and secular youth work, there is joint opportunity to figure out how best to work together on spiritual development for young people. Focus group participants and thought leaders from the Common Ground work requested an articulated framework that sorted through the definitions, narratives, and safe places where youth workers in all settings can create intentional dialogue about the issue of spirituality and articulate the differences. While this work needs to play out on the local level, national organizations can engage their local programs and encourage staff and youth to participate in intentional dialogue about the definitions and needed work going forward.

The associated practices and activities are not clear. In an effort to steer clear of religious activities, many youth workers and youth organizations that provide opportunities for spiritual development (for example, meditation or reflection; see the Promising Practices section of this volume) do not recognize them as spiritual or may be reluctant to label them spiritual for fear of retribution. Naming—naming emotions, naming skills, naming needs—is an important part of adolescent development. Not labeling these activities as spiritual, even if they are offered, makes it less likely that young people will have the opportunities for self-reflection or individual or group discussion that could make these activities more valuable.

Melanie Wilson compiled examples of religious and secular spiritual activities in *Practice Unbound.*[9] Religious activities included Bible or prayer groups, clergy programs, curriculum-based religious instruction, religious counseling, and religious rites-of-passage rituals. Secular spiritual activities included meditation, martial arts, yoga, guided visualization, musical expressions, and general rites of passage programs. Most of the "secular spiritual" activities Wilson summarized are closely associated with non-Christian religions. This finding reinforces the potential power of relabeling. These practices are already integrated into the activity menu of many youth organizations. Being more intentional, naming this as spiritual development and having it be an intended purpose and outcome, opens up opportunities for youth development staff to increase connection, contemplation, and dialogue with youth and support their exploration of who they are in relation to the larger universe and their spiritual selves.

In her 2004 study, Wilson found that teens identified simple everyday tasks and diversions as spiritual—things like "walking in the woods, talking with friends, listening to loud music, dancing, riding the bus, and even washing dishes." Each of these activities, for different reasons, can create an opportunity for transcendence—the state in which the self is embedded in or connected to something greater. As Wilson notes, youth workers and other adults can help teens see the spirituality in their lives by reframing these and other ordinary events that can develop their spiritual selves.[10]

The guidelines and supports for staff are not clear. For youth workers, spirituality is a lot like sexuality. Everyone experiences it, but most are uncomfortable talking to young people about it without explicit training, permission, and guidelines, and many are leery of others who do. The range of responses from faith-based and secular youth workers who were asked to define spirituality makes it clear why this discomfort exists. In focus groups conducted by the National Collaboration for Youth, the top answer was "relationship with God/Higher Power/Jesus Christ."[11] Many of the answers included some connection with religion: adoption of a religious doctrine, instilling religious traditions, Christian principles in practice, or Christian evangelism. Importantly, the second most frequent answer given by the American Camp Association survey participants was the importance of or connection with nature. Responses in both groups included definitions such as personal growth, learning, and connection with others and the universe. This fumbling with the articulation of a definition of spirituality once again points to the confusion between religion and spirituality.

Clearer distinctions will help, but deeper differences need repair to establish spiritual development as an important function for both faith-based and community-based institutions. One camp director articulated the problem clearly when discussing the challenges of joint training: "The greatest obstacle I see is the perception, whether accurate or not, that faith-based workers have their own agendas and that community-based workers lack a strong moral base."[12]

This obstacle not only makes it difficult for faith-based and secular workers to find common ground with each other; it makes it difficult for individual workers to know what the boundaries are. Forty-nine percent of the workers surveyed for the Common Ground study who work in secular settings described themselves as very religious, while 32 percent were somewhat religious. Without guidance and training that helps them understand the difference between religion and spirituality, these workers are likely to be conservative about bringing their spiritual selves into the workplace.[13]

The Common Ground survey found that community-based workers who defined themselves as very religious were twice as likely to respond that helping youth develop spiritually was an important part of their responsibilities. Even so, the percentage (20 percent) was still far below that reported by faith-based workers (77 percent). Wilson found that one quarter (26 percent) of the surveyed agencies gave "staff lacks expertise" as a reason for not offering secular spiritual training and one-sixth "staff might impose beliefs (17 percent)."[14]

Clearly there are workers whose knowledge and interest allow them to be comfortable taking risks. But because formal supports are lacking, the activities often stop when a particular worker leaves.[15] Training is needed, but the findings from the two surveys just discussed reinforce the conclusion that whatever their personal beliefs, community-based workers will be reluctant to discuss spirituality until signals are clear and supports available.

Lack of clarity about what spirituality is, where it can be formally claimed as a goal, how it can be supported through activities, and how much youth workers need to be trained and supported have most likely combined to suppress the number of workers and agencies interested in incorporating secular spiritual activities into their programs and stymie those who try. This is an unacceptable situation given the growing interest in supporting spiritual development.

Youth development and religion scholars need to curtail deliberations and offer the youth-serving community clear definitions of the process, outcomes, and contexts of spiritual development. Search Institute's assertive efforts to deliver on this goal are acknowledged. The question is, How should these definitions be delivered so that they not only inform debate but ignite commitments? Should they come in at the top with the directors of national organizations? In the middle with local executives? On the ground with youth workers? The answer, of course, is "all of the above." The emphasis, however, should be on engaging frontline workers across sectors.

Goal 2: Engaged champions

The climate is right to address each of these challenges directly. As Benson and Roehlkepartain note in their article opening this volume, there is growing evidence that spiritual development is quite salient for all young people and can be an important source of resilience for vulnerable youth. Moreover, there is significant interest among service providers in developing or expanding spiritual programming *if* the above issues can be addressed.

"Providers reported that they were uncertain about how to develop or expand spirituality programming for youth, how to evaluate such programs for effectiveness. In short, while agencies were intrigued . . . they wanted to know more."[16] The most effective way to jump-start this work may be to create cross-sector, cross-discipline learning and planning opportunities with youth workers, specifically with those who spend the majority of their time working directly with young people. We make this recommendation for three reasons: expediency, energy, and experience.

Expediency. Youth development is to youth-serving organizations as spirituality is to religion. To send a message that spirituality is central to youth development, we need first to engage the workers who work with youth. These are the paid and volunteer staff of youth development organizations—those focused on young people's social, civic, and physical development. But these workers are also employed by organizations that focus on academic, employment, and religious education and training (see Figure 2.1).

In the opening article, Benson and Roehlkepartain comment that the assertion that spiritual development is the province of the faith communities reinforces the problematic notion that different institutions have "exclusive responsibility for different parts of young people's development." They argue that if a wide range of youth development organizations decides to become more intentional about including spiritual development as part of their mandate, "it may open a dialogue across sectors that reinvigorates commitments to holistic development."

We agree, but it may be more expedient to start by engaging workers who are closer to where the youth development action is (the center of "star" shown in Figure 2.1) rather than with the leaders of the organizations that are differentiated at its points. Youth workers move freely between types of organizations (including crossing the religious-secular line). They also have the raw materials needed to ignite change: energy and experience.

Energy. At an April 2007 convening in Indianapolis of community- and faith-based practitioners and thought leaders (by the National Collaboration for Youth, Search Institute, and The Lilly Endowment) as part of the Common Ground project, it became clear that the sense of urgency for getting answers and removing barriers lies more with those who spend their time with young people than with those whose focus is board members and funders. This is not to say that there is no interest, passion, or capacity at the top to address this issue, but that

Figure 2.1. The youth development "star"

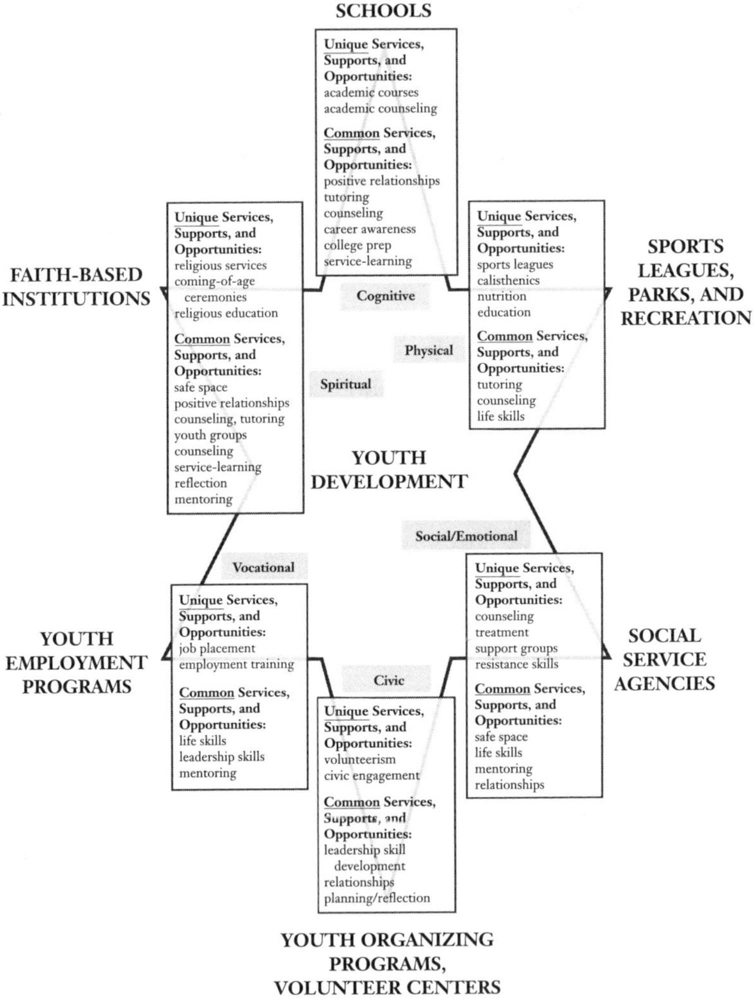

Source: Adapted from presentations made by K. Pittman, Forum for Youth Investment, 2004–2007.

those closest to young people are also closest to finding the solution because they see the consequences of not doing so.

The Common Ground survey found large differences between the percentages of religious- versus community-based youth workers who believed that helping young people develop spiritually was an essential component of their job (77 versus 14 percent). (*Spirituality* was not defined in the survey.) The differences between the percentages who were interested in receiving training, resources, or educational opportunities to develop this competence, however, were much closer: 56 versus 38 percent.[17]

Adding in a third factor, the extent to which workers already felt prepared to provide spiritual support, allows informed speculation. Only 8 percent of community-based youth workers felt well prepared compared to 27 percent of faith-based workers. Eighty-three percent of religious-based youth workers felt prepared or were interested in training to develop a competence that 77 percent felt essential to their jobs. But 46 percent of community-based workers felt prepared or were interested in being prepared to provide a support that is being required of only 14 percent of them. The energy lies inside this differential. If community-based workers are sent a signal that spiritual development is important, the response, on the basis of this survey, will be strong and positive.

Experience. Documentation of methods, activities, and curricula for supporting spiritual development is scarce, as Benson and Roehlkepartain note in the first article. But documentation is growing. Compilations of intentional strategies for supporting young people's spiritual development from the practices of both religious and secular programs have appeared in recent years. Examples range from case studies of the use of meditative breathing exercises coupled with the acting out of stories that require ethical solutions to descriptions of a formal curriculum for "welcoming soul into the classroom" that is used in schools and after-school programs.

Armed with clear definitions and rich examples of what they are looking for and permission to find and discuss it, frontline workers can simultaneously create a powerful demand for concrete experience-based examples and be a powerful force for not only filling the documentation void but also demonstrating the universality of certain spiritual development principles and practices.

Goal 3: Readiness assessments and engagement strategies

The arguments for responding to the call issued by the Commission on Children at Risk in *Hardwired to Connect* are overwhelming. The devil, however, is in the details of implementation. Progress can be made, but it is important to assess readiness of workers and organizations to proceed.

Youth worker readiness. The Common Ground survey and focus groups found that community-based and faith-based youth workers were equally interested in and excited about coming together to share, learn, and strengthen essential competencies. Fifty-seven percent were very interested. Only 5 percent were not interested.[18] There is a caveat, however. Youth workers from both sectors were afraid of being judged for their values and beliefs and were uncomfortable with the inclusion of religious or spiritual issues as topics for learning. Their desire was to focus cross-sector trainings on some of the core topics of youth development, for example, developing positive relationships with youth, involving and empowering youth, or interacting in ways that support asset building.

Readiness to find common ground across sectors does not equate with readiness to cross-train on spiritual development. This is an area where workers prefer to be trained separately. The direct approach is likely to backfire without a carefully laid foundation. But since there is ample evidence that faith-based and youth workers are eager to find common ground, it is possible for them to use this base to find common strategies for supporting spiritual development, especially if definitions and examples are accessible, concrete, and anchored between the bookends of religious development and moral development.

Youth organization readiness. The National Research Council's (NRC) definition of the key features of positive developmental settings sparked growth in program quality assessment tools that assess not the quality of the content or skill building but that of the learning environment created.[19] The NRC list had these features:

- Physical and psychological safety
- Appropriate structure

- Supportive relationships
- Opportunities to belong
- Positive social norms
- Support for efficacy and mattering
- Opportunities for skill building
- Integration of family, school, and community efforts

This list had an immediate impact on the field for two reasons. First, it became the Rosetta Stone against which all other youth development frameworks are now compared, from Search Institute's 40 Developmental Assets to America's Promise's 5 Promises. Second, in addition to defining the key features, the authors provide definitional anchors for each, describing contexts that could cause developmental harm and those associated with developmental growth.

Although this list was not specifically created to assess an organization's readiness to undertake the spiritual development of its young participants, it has considerable value. Not only does it signal a renewal of effort to define standards for youth programs, it provides a basis from which to assess the quality of any developmental setting where young people spend time.

Assessments of program quality conducted by the High/Scope Educational Research Foundation suggest that programs score fairly well on basic issues such as safety and structure, but poorly when it comes to critical developmental issues such as engagement and interactions.[20]

Given the perceived risks associated with expanding to include spiritual development, we should be cautious about encouraging youth-serving organizations to do so until they have demonstrated their general capacity to support youth development.

A young person from the Cathedral Home for Children, Laramie, Wyoming, states the challenge well: "How can someone explore their spirituality or look for a power greater than themselves, or pray, when you're telling them they don't even have a mind of their own . . . ? By giving them some freedom . . . you provide a lot more room for spiritual growth, to me, than another program would."[21]

Implications for action

A concerted effort to reissue the *Hardwired to Connect* challenge that opened this article would be not only well received but successful. Academics are responding to the need for clear, common definitions; youth organizations and youth workers are prepared to move forward if provided with the needed supports and assurances; and new definitions of high-quality developmental environments lend support to the inclusion of spiritual activities and outcomes.

Immediate steps can and should be taken to start the process:

- *Engage frontline workers across sectors.* Create cross-sector, cross-discipline learning and planning opportunities with youth workers who spend the majority of their time working directly with young people. Start with common ground topics to develop trust and increase cross-discipline knowledge. Stimulate and surface promising practices in spiritual development by asking workers to document their use of "secular" activities like meditation. Consider mounting a second Common Ground survey focused specifically on spiritual development, building on explicit definitions of outcomes, process, and activities.
- *Identify strategies for integrating spiritual development into youth work practice.* Provide youth and adults in community- and faith-based groups with clear definitions (and examples) of spiritual, religious, moral, and ethical development that underscore their commonalities and their differences, and encourage discussion. Then organize diverse, cross-sector study circles of frontline youth workers and youth for dialogue about how they understand and practice spiritual development, their hopes and fears around it, and the practices they use to cultivate it. Bring the groups together, potentially in dialogue with national leaders and young people, to share what worked for them and to shape an agenda for spiritual development in youth work.
- *Assess youth, youth worker, and organizational readiness.* Create supplements to widely used surveys and assessments of youth, youth worker practice, and organizational management that ask explicit

questions about spirituality (named, with a definition, and represented by specific practices, guidelines, and skills). Pilot their use among secular youth organizations already committed to improving quality. Explore options for piloting quality assessment of faith-based youth programs. Tools, promising practices, assessment measures, and intentional professional development opportunities need to be a crucial part of capitalizing on and improving readiness.

- *Build energy and commitment for making spiritual development an explicit goal.* Provide opportunities and incentives for youth development organizations on every level—local, state, regional, and national—to articulate the importance of spiritual development as a component of youth development closely linked to social development and civic engagement. Create alliances between organizations that focus on these three points of the star. Increase the presence of workshops, surveys, issue briefs, case studies, and practice guides on spiritual development and its interconnection with overall youth development.

Momentum is building. Concerted action to generate clarity, identify champions, and define and improve readiness should result in a significant increase in the availability of opportunities that, at a minimum, provide young people with the supports and the reflective space they need to develop their spiritual selves.

Notes

1. Commission on Children at Risk. (2003). *Hardwired to connect: The new scientific case for authoritative communities.* New York: Institute for American Values. P. 49.

2. Hay, D., Reich, K. H., & Utsch, M. (2005). Spiritual development: Intersections and divergence with religious development. In E. Roehlkepartain, P. Ebstyne King, L. Wagener, & P. Benson (Eds.), *The handbook of spiritual development in childhood and adolescence* (pp. 47–48). Thousand Oaks, CA: Sage.

3. Pittman, K., Irby, M., Tolman, J., Yohalem, N., & Ferber, T. (2003). Preventing problems, promoting development, encouraging engagement: Competing priorities or inseparable goals? Based on K. Pittman and M. Irby (1996), Preventing Problems or Promoting Development? (p. 11). Washington, DC: Forum for Youth Investment, Impact Strategies, Pittman, K. J., Irby,

M., Tolman, J., Yohalem, N., & Ferber, T. (2003, March). Preventing problems, promoting development, encouraging engagement: Competing priorities or inseparable goals? Washington, DC: The Forum for Youth Investment, Impact Strategies, Inc.

4. Templeton, J., & Eccles, J. (2005). The relation between spiritual development and identity process. In E. Roehlkepartain, P. Ebstyne King, L. Wagener, & P. Benson (Eds.), *The handbook of spiritual development in childhood and adolescence.* Thousand Oaks, CA: Sage. P. 254.

5. Wilson, M. (2004). *A part of you so deep: What vulnerable adolescents have to say about spirituality.* Burlington, VT: New England Network for Child, Youth and Family Services.

6. Garza, P., Artman, S., & Roehlkepartain, E. C. (2007). *Is there common ground? An exploratory study of the interests and needs of community-based and faith-based youth workers* (pp. 16–17). Washington, DC: National Collaboration for Youth, and Minneapolis, MN: Search Institute.

7. Wilson, M. (2002). *Practice unbound: A study of secular spiritual and religious activities in work with adolescents.* Burlington, VT: New England Network for Child, Youth and Family Services. P. 41.

8. Garza et al. (2007). P. 36.

9. Wilson. (2002).

10. Wilson. (2004). Pp. 40–41.

11. Garza et al. (2007). P. 37.

12. Garza et al. (2007). P. 35.

13. Garza et al. (2007).

14. Wilson. (2002). P. 39.

15. Wilson. (2002).

16. Wilson, M. (2005). *Adolescent heart and soul: Achieving spiritual competence in youth-serving agencies.* Burlington, VT: New England Network for Child, Youth and Family Services. P. 5.

17. Garza et al. (2007).

18. Garza et al. (2007).

19. Eccles, J., & Gootman, J. A. (2003). *Community programs to promote youth development.* Washington, DC: National Academy Press.

20. Smith, C., & Hohmann, C. (2005). *Full findings from the youth program quality assessment validation study.* Ypsilanti, MI: High/Scope Educational Research Foundation.

21. Wilson. (2005). P. 17.

KAREN PITTMAN *is the executive director of the Forum on Youth Investment, Washington, D.C.*

PAMELA GARZA *is cochair of the Next Generation Youth Work Coalition.*

NICOLE YOHALEM *is program director at the Forum on Youth Investment, Washington, D.C.*

STEPHANIE ARTMAN *is a graduate student at University of Texas at Austin.*

The metaphors of curator and navigational guide illuminate potential roles and activities for youth workers in nurturing young people's spiritual development.

3

Spiritual development in faith communities and secular societies

John A. Emmett

EVERY DAY IN MY Australian home, I listen to rising concerns in our society about the role of religion, and hear a growing passion among people of all ages to embrace a new spirituality. Young people are not immune to this trend. Religion, it seems, is problematic for both the believer and the skeptic. The vast majority of young people in Australian society have not embraced a religion of any recognized form. They are areligious, the inheritors of the secular dream. Yet young people's spirituality is becoming more overt and normalized.

The rise of spirituality

Spirituality consists of those philosophies and practices through which a person or community explores and seeks to make sense of experience. Usually spirituality is associated with being enlightened or becoming a better person. There is also a mystical dimension to

NEW DIRECTIONS FOR YOUTH DEVELOPMENT, NO. 118, SUMMER 2008 © WILEY PERIODICALS, INC.
Published online in Wiley InterScience (www.interscience.wiley.com) • DOI: 10.1002/yd.255

spirituality that some people associate with the notion of a being or force beyond humanity, which might include awareness of or encounter with a "transcendent other," a "divine" or "god" or "goddess" or "spirit." Spirituality connects an individual with meaning, values, and ethics, on the one hand, and on the other links an individual to community, and perhaps both individual and community to the transcendent.[1]

Since the Enlightenment, Western civilizations have moved steadily toward secularization. Religion and state have been separated to lesser or greater degrees, depending on what style of democracy has evolved. One result is that spirituality has become increasingly detached from religion.[2] Once religion may have given rise to and defined spirituality as an essential element of its worldview through particular philosophies and practices. Today spirituality, set adrift from its religious roots, is more difficult to define and describe. It has tended to become the domain of individualized definition, and therefore of individualized authority.

There are, of course exceptions to this trend. In some societies and subcultures, enculturation into the spiritual philosophies and practices of a specific religious tradition continues to be an essential function of adults responsible for raising young people. Where individuals' rights to freedom of choice are enshrined by law, such enculturation may be perceived as pejorative or as indoctrination by a society.

Youth subcultures and spirituality

It is not surprising that so many Western young people find religious affiliation unpalatable. Traditional, organized religions have largely failed to recognize and connect with the spirituality of young people. While some Eastern and Asian religions may appear to have sustained their ancient forms and mysticism, they attract a slowly growing but statistically small body of young people.[3] However, if adults take time to observe, they might recognize some evidence of a thriving spirituality in the diverse philosophies and practices of youth subcultures. For example, consider the following phenomena:

- Graffiti art is sprayed with intentional design on walls, trains, and bus shelters. Anthems of the moment beat out from personal earphones into public space. Diverse styles of clothing bedecked with cryptic messages proclaim meaning, and brands depict symbols of belonging.
- Young athletes strive for bodily and performance perfection, attempting to solve the mystery of human capacity. The pain of rejection and alienation of so many inner-city young people is obvious to those who will see it arising from their body language. Young people enthusiastically communicate their dreams for an overseas trip before they get a job, find a long-term partner, and settle down. It is a pilgrimage as much as an exercise in self-discovery as geographical exploration.[4]
- Many young people dabble in mysteries and explore numerous rituals. They carry talismans and collect symbols. Academically equipped young people assert the supposed truth of their learning, striving to push the previous generation out of the way to claim what they consider rightfully their own.
- Young lyricists, musicians, playwrights, and actors strut their stuff on the boards of TV reality shows, local pubs, and festivals. They are drumming out their search for and discoveries about meaning for all who will perceive it.

What will it look like?

The Western world is experiencing a spirituality revolution.[5] How are we to understand this revolution, this highly energized search for the spiritual in respect to the development of a young person, and to a community of young people? Where are the people who relate strongly with or work with young people with respect to this spirituality revolution?

Describing the priorities of youth workers in both secular and faith-based settings in the United States, the 2007 Common Ground report has noted that only a very small percentage of youth workers in community-based organizations assess themselves interested, let alone competent, to engage young people in their own spiritual development.[6] Yet other research suggests that almost half of U.S. young people surveyed indicated that their religious beliefs are extremely important in shaping their major life decisions.[7] Recognizing the anomaly the United States reveals with respect to the religiosity of young people, the research findings remind us that religious participation does not equate or transfer directly to spiritual development. How can youth workers, whether faith based or secular, respond to the spiritual development needs of young people, yet do so without pursuing a particular religious institution's prescribed pathways for doing so?

Definitions provide useful starting points in clarifying what it is that youth workers might do in engaging the spiritual development of young people. In the opening article of this volume, Benson and Roehlkepartain propose that spiritual development may involve the dynamic interplay of at least three developmental processes: awareness or awakening, interconnecting and belonging, and a way of living.

The definition provides for a common ground between secular and faith-based spiritual development, and thus forms a basis for imagining new roles for youth workers. This definition also invites a dynamic understanding of spiritual development and implies that development might be thought of as movement. Drawing on the insights of many formalized spiritualities, we can suggest a basic four-step movement to be used to assist young people to engage their own spiritual development: noticing, or attending; inquiring; interpretation; and action.[8]

Attending, or noticing, focuses one's attention on the experience at hand. Various religious and nonreligious institutions and philosophical and psychological schools of thought and practice have developed simple practices to attend. These include breathing in certain ways, assuming physical postures, and shutting down the more dominant senses to concentrate the less dominant. As one becomes acutely aware through engaging in such an exercise, one is free to notice many features of the experience encountered.

Having noticed, one is free to begin inquiring into what has been noticed. Again there are many forms of meditative or contemplative practices in both secular and religious traditions that provide processes by which to conduct an inquiry of a particular experience. In addition, psychology and other social sciences can provide more analytical methods of inquiry.

Third is interpretation. An inquiry will have produced data of one sort or another. Interpretation is the process of sifting and assembly to make sense of the data.

Finally, an individual gains insight, sensing new meanings and purpose, that learning and development lead to action, likely with observable changes to disposition and behavior. Over time, these changes might bring one to conclude that a young person had indeed been engaging in the processes of spiritual development.

Equipping young people to notice, inquire, and interpret helps them to develop a sense of meaning and purpose, leading to involvement and contribution. In this way, informed, skilled youth workers assist a young person to develop personal awareness of spirituality and make sense of life experiences.

To help adults who are in serious life-shaping relationships with young people to recognize and respond to their spiritual development, I propose two metaphors for different roles for youth workers:

- Youth workers as curators
- Youth workers as navigational guides

Youth workers as curators

A visit to the local museum or art gallery is enhanced by an encounter with the curator. Curators curate the collected knowledge about the artifacts and often communicate the wisdom that surrounds the collection.

For example, in Canberra, the national capital of Australia, the National War Memorial Museum houses an extensive collection of artifacts relevant to the various wars in which Australians have been involved. In addition to armaments and hardware, the museum houses artworks, letters of soldiers, battle plans, and extensive commentary by historians about the battles and wars fought. Curators conserve and add to the collection, provide accessibility to the collection, and explain and assist persons in making sense of their experience with the collection. In the process, curators also connect with the values the collection represents, offering possible interpretations of the artifacts with which the viewer seeks to engage. The curator is not values neutral in such an engagement, but can act in an objective manner with respect to comments made and perspectives introduced.

Youth workers can be curators of a community's spirituality. As curators they will provide access to the artifacts of various cultures' spirituality. The artifacts of any community's spirituality might include the following: music and other sounds; objects; places and journeys; and festivals, rituals, and special seasons.

Music and other sounds

Music has aroused great passion in every era, for example, national anthems, or songs and music associated with particular causes. Religious traditions use hymns or psalms, chants, and choirs. Secular traditions also use music extensively, developing anthems including lyrics and music designed to stir the spirit.

Sounds and repeated patterns of speech are often associated with particular meanings, often accompanied by movement—for example, indigenous or national dances, or the threatening Haka war dance of the Maori people of Aotearoa, New Zealand. The stirring mix of myth, sound, and kinetic energy reaches deep into the spirit of any New Zealander. For Buddhists and Hindus, the primordial om or aum signals an entry into meditation. Muslim, Jewish, and other traditions also use mantras as a process for initiating spiritual meditation. In a secular setting, major league games and international events are often begun or closed with music, anthems, and particular sounds associated with deeply held meanings by those attending or participating.

Objects

Visual items have frequently assumed a symbolic value in various cultures and subcultures, such as logos, talismans, and regional, national, or political symbols. Films can also be perceived as presenting and preserving visual matters of symbolic value.

For Australians, the sight of the red kangaroo on the tail of the QANTAS airplanes is a sign of home, a symbol of safety and reliability. For Christians, the bread and wine associated with Holy Communion evoke the deepest sense of belonging. For Buddhists, the Dalai Lama is a visual symbol of transcendence. The colors of a particular sporting team can become symbolic; on sporting teams' clothing, colors stand for particular values, beliefs, meanings, and behaviors to supporters.

Places and journeys

Every culture identifies special places in which people may experience a sense of the transcendent or sacred. Celtic Christian tradition identifies such places as "thin places"—those locations where the sacred seems to break through or appears to be more easily accessed by questing individuals. When questioned about such places, Australians often comment about the outback—the inland dry, deserted wilderness regions of our continent—or the sea; we seem to be either "bush" or "beach" people. Religious traditions have long considered natural wilderness as a special place in which the transcendent or sacred might be encountered.

Where do young people find such "thin" places? Cities often fail to provide the possibility of regular and frequent contact with wilderness places. Increasingly spirituality in respect to special places is difficult for young people, except through camp experiences (see the article in this volume by Karla A. Henderson and M. Deborah Bialeschki).

Attention to architecture sometimes provides a special place for some young people. Cathedrals inspire a sense of being beyond awareness of oneself. Mosques inspire confidence in a holy other. Both religious and secularly disposed young people may find inspiration in the fine design of an art gallery or a public space created in an inner-city square, park, or garden.

Journeys to special places connect a young person to her or his origins or to stories that have assumed mythical status in explaining the origins of their nation. Such journeys can be called pilgrimages. For example, many young Australians make a pilgrimage to ANZAC Cove in Turkey to connect with the Australian soldiers and sailors who died there, sustaining a myth about the birth of the Australian character. Many Muslims dream of a pilgrimage to Mecca. Christians retrace the steps and pathways of great saints, such as the Spanish Camino.

Festivals, rituals, and special seasons

Consider particular times and associated rituals, such as regional, indigenous, cultural, or national festivals—for example, Thanksgiving Day celebrations in the United States and Canada, and for me, Australia Day (January 26), which for nonindigenous Australians celebrates the arrival of the First Fleet in 1788. For indigenous Australians, May 26 marks National Sorry Day, a day to remember the act of European invasion and the terrors visited on their nation groups by subsequent waves of invasion. Young people raised in religious faiths observe times of remembrance and celebration, such as Easter for Christians and Yom Kippur for Jews.

Special seasons, extended periods when particular festivals or celebrations occur, might reflect religious meanings, have deep cultural significance, or hold ethnic significance. For example, Ramadan is a special season for Muslims. In a secular vein in Australia, Schoolies' Week is a special season of celebration for young people who have completed their secondary education with an exhausting spate of final examinations.

Using the artifacts of spirituality

The story, imagery, and symbolism associated with any artifact contribute to the dimensions of culture or society's spirituality. A skilled curator can make these features accessible to a young person. Wise youth workers, either faith based or secular, make themselves aware of the artifacts of the spirituality that surrounds and nurtures the young persons in their care.

Prudent exposure to and engagement with the artifacts of spirituality in the context of supportive and positive relationships with trusted adults enable a young person to explore various dimensions of spirituality.[9] A well-informed youth worker, acting with skilled objectivity, can avoid indoctrination, by intention or neglect, to help a young person try various ideas or weigh alternative ways of expressing spirituality.

But it is not enough to know about the practices of spirituality; a youth worker must also know of the practice of spirituality by personal experience. Personal and institutional values are deeply embedded in the approach as much as in the content of any attempt to inform, form, or introduce transformative experiences to another person or group. With self-knowledge, skilled and scholarly inquiry methods, data, and stories about spirituality, youth workers can maintain objectivity by exposing the artifacts as well as meanings and values derived from them, to open, informed inquiry.

Workers with young people as navigational guides

Youth culture throughout the Western world is exhibiting a crisis of social meaning. It is critical that young people know how to navigate the many issues that contribute to a holistic human development. Operating as navigational guides, youth workers can offer young persons guidance in their spiritual development.

Navigators have played significant roles in geographical, oceanographic, aeronautical, and outer-space discovery. Using a range of instruments, as well as the natural phenomena of earth, waters, and sky, navigators have acquired a deep and detailed knowledge of our world and helped explorers and travelers alike find their way in unfamiliar surroundings. As guides, navigators rely on the findings of earlier explorers as well as their own experiences. To be a navigator is to point others to a path and know how to find the necessary bearings along the way.

When a youth worker adopts the role of a navigational guide, he or she may engage in activities such as assisting young people in these ways:[10]

- Finding their spiritual bearings
- Checking out their own and other people's community traditions
- Listening to the spiritual sonar from other people's experiences
- Interpreting their radar or sonar's messages of spirituality from sources beyond their community's experience

Getting one's bearings is about helping young people to locate themselves in respect to spiritual development. For example, a youth worker could assist a young person in checking whether his or her interpretation of a particular experience makes sense:

- Is my experience typical of that of other people?
- Can other people understand what I have related to them about my experience?
- Do people in other places, and even of other times, report similar experiences and meanings?
- How has this experience helped me to grow as a person?
- In what ways might this experience assist me to make a valuable contribution to the communities to which I belong?

Asking such questions may help a young person recognize that an experience has a spiritual dimension.

Helping a young person explore the meaning others have made of experiences in the past calls for validating the community's traditions. For example, all communities assemble a great deal of tradition—a pool of common sense, or public domain–styled meaning. If there is some sense of resonance between the tradition and the young person's experience of the spirit, then perhaps he or she can be aware of personal spiritual development.

Faith-based traditions offer their adherents or followers pathways that may include scriptures or sacred writings, stories, patterns of socialization, ethical guidelines for relationships, and rituals. They also provide teachings, usually couched in doctrinal or dogmatic form, as well as a learning pedagogy and method. In addition, each religious tradition has developed pathways, or disciplines, to explore and develop in the apprehension of mystery.[11]

Spirituality does not offer structured or predictable traditions in the same way as a faith-based religion does. Spiritual traditions may be more about practice, or method, than offering a coherent worldview. This is one reason that a young person may require a youth worker acting as a navigational guide, who instructs the young person how to navigate spirituality with purpose and affective and cognitive understanding.

Many sources of spirituality offer experiences or encounters with the transcendent. Some sources are accessible through other people, who guide their friends into similar encounters to those that they have experienced. When youth workers guide a young person to listen to and read messages from beyond the experience of her or his own community, she or he listens and reads to the ping of his or her own spirituality sonar. (Perhaps it is this approach to spiritual development that parents, youth workers, and social worker are most concerned about. In particular, it is precisely this phenomenon that religious fundamentalists and sects often apply in recruiting new members. However, if youth workers guide young persons toward a diversity of life experience in which the possibility of spiritual encounter is upheld, then it is more likely that fundamentalist entrapment will be identified and rejected.)

Listening to a close friend or an author retelling accounts of her or his personal encounters with the mysterious or of spirituality mediated through one's own life experience provides a young person with a peer relationship in which to reflect on her or his own experiences. Such conversation enables a natural sharing of meaning making and can contribute to a shared sense of the spiritual.[12]

Within some religious traditions, sharing personal stories is known as the practice of testimony. Across secular communities, sharing stories of meaning making can embrace a wide range of practices and settings. For example, Australian public bars have always been the natural home of "bush balladeers." Their stories cradled within their fabric the spirituality of an emerging and independent nation, and they continue to do so now, embracing skilled practitioners of various age groups and cultures. Young people exposed to such practices, whether in intimate and cozy pub rooms or when assembled in public spaces, are invited to use their sonar to detect the threads of spirituality that contribute to self-transcendence.

Radio-telescopes help people to see beyond their immediate context, to see farther and highlight what at first seems distant and indistinct. Reading the scope is a metaphor for young people developing spiritually when they recognize that there are many ways to make sense of spiritual encounters and diverse ways to understand self-transcendence. Sometimes religious institutions can assist spiritual development by maintaining an open and inquiring stance to the spiritual and spirit. Rather than taking dogmatic or doctrinaire approaches, they encourage scholarly inquiry, open discussion, and diverse but informed opinions. In secular settings, literature and art may serve a similar function.

For some young people, the discovery that there are values that reach beyond the immediate and specific needs of an egocentric human being propels them toward perceiving the world very differently. (This is one reason that service-learning is such a favored approach to forming the values of teenagers; see the article in this volume by Liane J. Louie-Badua and Maura Wolf.) The truths that such insights bring can shape the direction of the emerging adult's life. Young persons, guided by their youth workers, acquire skills by which to listen to the sonar of others' experiences and see beyond themselves and their immediate life setting. By so doing they may well develop commitments that embed values in their daily lives.

Engaging in the roles of curator and navigational guide, youth workers can make an essential contribution to the spiritual development of young people, which may be a critical factor in determining a thriving, holistic adult person who engages fully with her or his community, whether faith based or secular, to the developmental benefit of all involved.

Notes

1. See, for example, Johnson, S. (1989). *Christian spiritual formation in the church and classroom.* Nashville, TN: Abingdon; Bass, D. (1997). *Practicing our faith.* San Francisco: Jossey-Bass; Tacey, D. (2003). *The spirituality revolution—the emergence of contemporary spirituality.* New York: HarperCollins (see in particular Chapter Two).

2. See, for example, Cox, H. (1965). *The secular city: Secularization and urbanization in theological perspective.* New York: Collier Books.

3. Hughes, P. (2007). *Putting it together: Findings from Australian youth spirituality research.* Fairfield, CT: Fairfield Press.

4. See Ault, N. (2001). Spiritual life as a journey: A metaphor of exclusion? *Journal of Christian Education, 44*(1), 29–37.

5. Tacey. (2003).

6. Garza, P., Artman, S., & Roehlkepartain, E. C. (2007). *Is there common ground? An exploratory study of the interests and needs of community-based and faith-based youth workers.* Washington, DC: National Collaboration for Youth, and Minneapolis, MN: Search Institute.

7. Smith, C., with Denton, M. L. (2005). *Soul searching: The religious and spiritual lives of American teenagers.* New York: Oxford University Press. Hughes, in *Putting It Together* (p. 148), notes that "a group of around 15% of Australian young people were involved in religion and passionate about it. The majority were not deeply concerned."

8. Ault, N. (2005). Envisioning a systems-based spirituality for lifelong Christian education. *Colloquium, 37*(1), 45–67. Ault draws on and applies this concept of movement to the notion of spirituality as a journey.

9. Hughes. (2007). Pp. 165ff.

10. I first encountered the navigational metaphor in respect to one human being encouraging the development of another in Sweet, L. (1999). *Aqua church: Essential leadership arts for piloting your church in today's fluid culture.* Denver, CO: Group Publishing.

11. Taken together, these six dimensions contribute to the structure of an organized religion. Smart, N. (1975). *What is religion? New movements in religious education.* London: Temple Smith. Pp. 13–22.

12. Dean, K. C., & Foster, R. (1998). *The Godbearing life: The art of soul tending for youth ministry*. Nashville, TN: Upper Room Books. This book devotes a chapter to discussing how a circle of friends shapes and nourishes the spiritual growth of a young person.

JOHN A. EMMETT *is a Christian educator working as a community development catalyst with the Uniting Church, Synod of Victoria and Tasmania, Australia.*

The origin of youth work in religious good works in the United Kingdom now shapes the role of spirituality in the profession.

4

Putting spiritual development of young people on the map: An English perspective

Maxine Green

SPIRITUALITY, as Benson and Roehlkepartain say in the opening article, provokes strong reactions in any field, and when this subject is coupled with young people, a further range of issues and concerns is raised.

In this article I look at some of the issues that are currently active in the United Kingdom when young people and spirituality are discussed:

- Defining spirituality
- Understanding whether it is community or individually based
- Understanding spirituality within a progress paradigm in education
- Measuring spirituality
- Seeing where the youth workers' own spirituality has an impact on their work with young people
- Looking at the risks around doing this sort of work
- Acknowledging that spirituality can be bad as well as good

NEW DIRECTIONS FOR YOUTH DEVELOPMENT, NO. 118, SUMMER 2008 © WILEY PERIODICALS, INC.
Published online in Wiley InterScience (www.interscience.wiley.com) • DOI: 10.1002/yd.256

Defining spirituality

One key issue emerging in the debate is that of language and definition. A search for a definition of *spirituality* unearths a range of personal dynamics that are deeply and profoundly held. This concept cannot be discussed using only analytical thought and rationality; it is complex and involves emotions, values, and aspirations. There is real struggle in trying to pin down a definition of *spirituality* and *spiritual development* and yet a real need to identify and agree on the concept if it is to be promoted and used in education.

The complexity of the subject became evident when I embarked on producing the publication *A Journey of Discovery*.[1] It started with a commission from the U.K. government's Department for Education and Skills to write a book that looked at spirituality and spiritual development in youth work. My first reaction was elation at being chosen to do this, quickly followed by a sense of the overwhelming nature of the task and an awareness of the minefield around spirituality and religion in youth work currently.

However, it was a necessary task and challenge, and I undertook it. The key areas I tried to address in this work were defining spirituality and spiritual development. I interviewed a range of young people and those who work with young people, held focus groups, and undertook an extensive consultation exercise. The three core areas that Benson and Roehlkepartain identified in the opening article—awareness or awakening, interconnecting and belonging, and owning a way of living—resonate with my findings. (It is particularly important that they have included contact with "the other," broadly represented as a transcendental God, for if the "God" part is left out, much of what they are suggesting could be termed *social and emotional literacy*.)

The term *spiritual* is not going to fit neatly into a definition, and we may need to use a linguistic perspective to move forward. Jean Aitchinson, a notable English linguist, talks of "fuzzy concepts," which elude precise definition but around which there is a shared understanding of what is meant.[2] Concepts such as love, wonder, faith, and spirituality, rather than being strictly defined, are better served through a process of sharing our understandings.

One exercise I used to elucidate the term *spiritual* was to draw a target on a flip chart and invite people to write associated thoughts, feelings, and actions on the chart. The nearer they thought the terms were to the target understanding of *spiritual*, the closer they put them to the bull's-eye. This produced some extremely interesting debates, but the exercise also revealed much common understanding and agreement about what *spiritual* means.

Exercises like this also showed how the term *spiritual* is held at a core identity level by some people. For example at a meeting following the preparation of the consultation paper that preceded *A Journey of Discovery*, one of the participants spoke vehemently and angrily about how the words *spiritual* and *spiritual development* had no place in the youth work curriculum. His opinion was that this opened the door for irrational thought and manipulative practices of religious organizations. It transpired in a conversation afterward that he had had some extremely bad experiences with a fundamentalist religious denomination in his youth that had deeply affected him, which helped to explain his vehemence as well as his legitimate points of concern.

A further perspective is offered by members of different faiths who cannot understand how spirituality can possibly exist out of a religious context. I drew an absolute blank with a Muslim taxi driver who was unable to understand spirituality as a free-standing concept that can exist outside a religious life. In the research, it became evident that the three concepts of spirituality, religion, and faith are inextricably linked, and it is vital that there be clear working definitions of these three areas.

When I was asked in 1999 to be the guest editor on spirituality for the journal *Youth and Policy*, I asked John Hull, the English theologian, to try to unravel the dynamic between faith, religion, and spirituality. The model he used to explain the relationships was three concentric circles. He argued that for some people, religion was in the inner circle, with faith in the next circle; for others, faith was central, with religion as the next concentric circle. In both models, faith and religion, he argues, are subsumed in the concept of spirituality: "Spirituality . . . is the achievement of humanness, and the religions are the traditions and techniques for achieving this in relation to the transcendent Ultimate. Faith, however, has to do with subjectivity. It is the positive human response to the issues raised by spirituality."[3]

As soon as words are put on the page, issues arise. For example, Quakers speak of "the light within," which is not immediately reconcilable with Hull's idea of the transcendent ultimate, and this definitely falls outside the worldview of a humanist or atheist. In exploring the whole issue one of the interesting areas that John Hull noted in his article was the way the word *spirit* is used:

> The same is true of the spiritual. When we speak of the spirit of a sporting team, we refer to some quality of the behavior and attitudes of the team as a whole, and the same is true of the "spirit of the nation", "the spirit of war" and so on. In such expressions we do not refer to a part of the whole, but to some energizing and invigorating quality of the whole.

This use of *spirit* also connects with the European perspective, where youth workers are sometimes called *animateurs*, as they animate and enliven young people.

All of this points to the need for agreeing on the terms that form the parameters of the debate and constructing a definition matrix that has both a theistic and a nontheistic dimension.

My journey or a community response?

A Muslim youth worker explained that faith, religion, and spirituality are so bound together in the Islamic idea of community and service that personal spiritual development runs contrary to the idea of promoting society. The individual perspective is so important in framing Western thinking that it is difficult to access other ways of perceiving the world, so we can find ourselves in a similar position to the Muslim taxi drivers as we in the West try to see the world with a communal frame. Individual progress, achievement, and growth are the foundation of our education systems, and this paradigm is also present when we look at spiritual development. This is coupled with the concept of the rights of the individual rather than a more community-based approach where the good of society is paramount.

The community dimension of spirituality that is illustrated in all faith traditions does not fit within the individual progressive paradigm. Where individuals are positioned at the center of education theory, group tasks and group development sit uneasily. What is evident from my research is that youth work involves young people in groups, so that any spiritual work is bound to have a community and sharing element.

Youth work within a convergent educational value system

In England at present, much work with young people across different faiths is framed as contributing to social cohesion and building a more inclusive society. A principal driver for this work is fear of extremism and a concern that this extremism is fueled by religious belief.

Over the past fifteen years, there has been a strong trend in the educational movement to focus on behavior, skills, and competence with a view to producing active citizens who can contribute economically and socially. This has further marginalized educational practice, which is value driven, with a corresponding effect on spiritual and religious work. In addition, many of the targets that are currently being set for youth workers are aimed at turning young people who are NEET (not in education, employment, or training) into those who are EET (in education, employment, or training). Youth workers and other professionals have been creative in using voluntary, relationship-based work as a tool to enable them to meet their targets, but there has been an organizational push to change youth work methodology into a more outcome-driven approach. A subject area such as spirituality is an obvious victim when this more convergent approach is used. Spiritual aims and achievements are notoriously difficult to measure, so it is easier to count more straightforward outcomes.

This educational approach, which rates behavior higher than values and knowledge, runs contrary to the historical and philosophical roots of youth work in which values are the focus and drivers for change. Classic youth work is voluntary and predicated on the principle that the young person is in control and has the resources or can get the resources he or she needs, and the role of the youth worker is to facilitate this process. The youth work process starts with valuing the whole young person, cognizant of his or her beliefs and values, including spirituality. There is an inherent expectation and trust that the decisions young people make, because they are rooted in their values and identity, will lead to appropriate and healthy behavior.

Different interested parties have been debating these issues, and one of the battlegrounds in the United Kingdom has been the drawing up of professional and national occupational standards. When the standards were formulated about five years ago, spirituality was framed as a potentially negative influence, and the draft standards protected young people against religious manipulation. These early drafts were changed after consultation with youth workers involved in faith organizations so that spirituality was seen as a potentially positive dimension of youth work.

The debate went back and forth, with some drafts emerging without the word *spirituality* included, followed by other drafts with the word in. The penultimate revision of these occupational standards involved a focused campaign by the Christian youth work sector to ensure that spirituality featured in the standards. The final standards, developed by Lifelong Learning UK, which is licensed by the U.K. governments to produce such standards, now have an element titled, "Encourage the spiritual development of young people, which encompasses understanding their own values, beliefs, emotions and feelings and enabling young people to respect other ethical, moral, cultural and belief systems." (The complete standards can be found at http://www.lifelonglearninguk.org.)

The discussion over these standards reflects the ambivalent attitude and approach to faith and spirituality. On the one hand, the government recognizes the necessity of including people's religious belief and value systems. On the other hand is a deep fear that promoting religion in educational settings may encourage fanatical belief and extremist actions.

The developmental aspect of spiritual development also needs attention in the debate. In most other fields, development is inexorably linked with progress and gaining more. Interestingly, many metaphors that chart the spiritual journey center on the idea of stripping away, or refining. The spiritual journey is often an elegant one where superfluous ideas, feelings, and actions drop away as people move on.

Measuring spirituality

In the United Kingdom, work is often commissioned and paid for on the basis of results and specified outcomes. For spiritual work to be commissioned, it must demonstrate significant, measurable outcomes. A leader of a major organization that works with young people asked me what the demonstrable outcomes were for spiritual development, implying that without outcomes, no funding could follow. Concern about measuring spirituality is valid, for it is primarily about values, and most measurements apply to behavior and knowledge. Although behavior and knowledge may indicate the state of people's values, they are a poor way of assessing a spiritual position.

In the research for *Journey of Discovery*, when I broached the possibility of measuring spirituality, some of my interviewees were horrified and deeply resistant. This usually had to do with their understanding of spirituality as being special or sacred. There was also a feeling expressed that this was one area that could not be prodded, poked, and manipulated by authority, giving further energy to their hands-off position.

My own position is one of uncertainty. If spirituality could be measured, it could take its part as a central and significant part of the educational curriculum. As a result funding, resourcing, and training would follow so that young people would have more opportunity to explore their spirituality. Yet I feel deep unease at the thought of people who lack the necessary sensitivity and competence being responsible for the measurement of spirituality, and I can foresee a reductionist and soul-shriveling methodology being invented.

Perhaps the winning position is for spirituality to be included in the curriculum for young people as a divergent, exploratory option that is devoid of the constraints of formal education.

Youth workers' own spiritual journey

Another important area is the competence and confidence of youth workers to work with spirituality with young people. In England currently, a number of organizations are training youth workers to work in a religious context, for example, the Centre for Youth Ministry and the Muslim Youthwork Foundation. There is also work on spirituality undertaken by organizations such as the Baha'i, who run projects with schools and other secular organizations to help children and young people with their personal, social, and spiritual development. However, given that spirituality is part of the youth work curriculum, there is a pressing need for youth workers to explore this area of work. A recent funding application was put together by a number of organizations working in this area to pilot and build a program and range of resources to support and train youth workers. Central to it is the youth worker's own spiritual understanding and recognition of their own spiritual journey.

Being able to reflect on one's own spiritual journey and position is hugely important when working with others. In the same way that counselors need to have been in analysis themselves so that they can identify and manage issues of transference, spiritual work needs to be similarly grounded. A lack of personal reflection on the part of those working with young people is potentially damaging and harmful.

"Bad spirituality" as well as good

It became apparent through the consultation that there is a need to be open to the concept of "bad spirituality." During my time as national youth officer of the Church of England, I came across many young people who were survivors of the zealous manipulative youth work practices of some Christian organizations. For some young people, the effect of this was relatively mild, and although they may have been pushed out of a community for daring to air their doubts, they could move on and recover. For others, there was more damage. One respondent was a mother who had been completely rejected by her son: "I have personal issues with churches that brainwash young people when they are vulnerable, as a local Evangelist Church has done with my oldest son (18). . . . They have actually taught him that I, his own mother, am evil because I do not work in their way, and if he ever talks to me it is only to try desperately to save my soul by converting me."[4]

Bad spirituality can happen as a result of perversion and contortion of intrinsically good religious or faith positions. The Muslim community has considerable concern about the power of faith in cultivating extremist attitudes in the young, a concern shared by other faiths and the government. It can also happen when young people are exposed to dangerous or bad belief systems such as Satanism. For professionals working in the field, there needs to be a way of assessing competence to understand and deal with spirituality and a way of assessing spiritual values against the broad positive values of the society.

Risk factors

A further important context is the way that society is increasingly risk averse, especially in relation to children and young people. Recent legislation in England entitled Every Child Matters was prompted by the sad and cruel death of a young child, Victoria Climbie, at the hands of her caregivers. The principal aim of this legislation is to protect children and young people, and consequently the departments that have overall responsibility for working with children and young people place a huge emphasis on their social care and safety. So it is not surprising that the aim of developing young people has gotten a bit lost. Education is seen as being the work of extended schools, and youth work and youth services have been pushed to the margins. "Risky" work such as outdoor education is on the decline as fewer teachers and youth workers are prepared to risk their jobs and possible court cases for the rewards of taking young people on trips.

This risk aversion is also evident in relationships between youth workers and young people. Youth workers have reported to me that they do not discuss spirituality with young people for fear of offending them. Many youth workers find the simplest option is to ignore the issue in their relationships with young people. Yet a key quality of youth work is its holistic and integrating nature, and excluding the spiritual severely damages the whole professional offer.

Putting spirituality on the map

Before spirituality can be taken seriously and included in legislation, policy, and practice, we need significant evidence that it is a good thing. One way to legitimize the inclusion of spirituality as part of the educational offer is by citing historical continuity, working on the principle that including spirituality has stood the test of time. Another way would be to align spirituality with the higher aspirational aims found in developmental theory, for example, Maslow's hierarchy of needs. It could also be argued that spirituality, when expressed as part of a faith or religion, has huge value at an individual, community, national, or international level, so to ignore such a powerful dynamic is foolish. The need for further research on the potency of spirituality at every level is clear.

Historical perspective

Citing the historical perspective is extremely useful for emphasizing the continuing importance of spirituality in work with young people. The following highlights of the early days of youth work in England demonstrate the continuity between some of the early pioneers and some work with young people today.

In 1844, the YMCA included in its Statement of Purpose a commitment to "the improvement of the spiritual and mental condition of young men." The YMCA was one of the first of many organizations committed to the development of young people. Many of these early organizations, like the YMCA, had a Christian foundation. While some had holistic aims for the development of the whole person, others were intent on converting young people to Christianity. As many of these movements were sponsored and supported by wealthy individuals for the benefit of the working classes, there were moral as well as spiritual aims for this work.

In 1942, the McNair Committee was appointed to consider the supply, recruitment, and training of teachers and youth leaders and to report what principles should guide these matters. In 1944 the McNair committee commented on the need for youth workers to act as "guides, philosophers and friends."[5] This builds on the importance of young people's values and beliefs as part of youth work process. And in 1951 Lord Redcliffe-Maud defined the aim of youth services as "to offer individual young people in their leisure time, opportunities of various kinds, complementary to those at home, formal education and work, to discover and develop their personal resources of body and mind and spirit and thus better equip themselves to live the life of mature creative and responsible members of the Free Society."[6]

This government support of including the spirit in the focus of youth work continued in the Albemarle Report, a watershed document in the history and professionalization of youth work, which held the youth service responsible for helping young people develop "a sense of fellowship," "the capacity to make sound judgments," and "mutual respect and tolerance."[7] More recently in 1998, David Blunkett, writing as the secretary of state for education and employment in *The Learning Age*, restated how learning develops a spiritual side in our lives: "As well as securing our economic future, learning has a wider contribution. It helps make ours a civilised society, develops a spiritual side of our lives and promotes active citizenship. It strengthens the family, the neighbourhood and consequently the nation."[8]

There were also influences on education from the contact that Britain had across the world over the previous century. The charismatic Indian educator Rabindranath Tagore says, "We may become powerful by knowledge, but we attain fullness by sympathy. The highest education is that which does not merely give us information but makes our lives in harmony with existence.[9]

In the United Kingdom, the worldwide scout movement was influenced by early educational pioneers in England and India. This in turn fed into a strong and well-developed branch of youth work called outdoor education. As the scout movement expects young scouts to have a relationship with God or the divine, outdoor education has always had elements of reflection and spiritual experience as well as the physical aims and benefits.

All of these individuals and their education theories have built a bedrock for British youth work, but the relationship between education and religion has not been straightforward and unproblematic. Since the 1960s, there has been considerable argument concerning the role of religion and faith in state provision. In the 1970s, when Prime Minister Margaret Thatcher famously proclaimed that there was "no such thing as society," value-driven work of all sorts, including religious or spiritual, was out of fashion. But this should not stop those who share the values of Rabindranath Tagore to continue to promote spirituality for the deeper intrinsic reasons of becoming fully human.

Young people as agents of change

Young people's participation or active involvement has spread as an expectation in the workings of local government. Many agencies across the United Kingdom are using the National Youth Agency's excellent document *Hear by Right* and adopting the recommendations within it.[10] One of the early stages illustrated there is that when organizations shift their perspective, they move from seeing young people as individuals benefiting from their contact to realizing that young people can make a significant contribution to improving local services.

This shift parallels my own realization that young people's understanding of the spiritual can offer the wider society a fresh and nonjaded approach. The whole energy of the consultation endeavor changed when I saw young people's power as agents of change in their own spiritual development. There emerged the possibility that young people had potent messages that could benefit society, even if society tended to ignore them. My understanding now is that these messages could be particularly useful to faith organizations, as many are struggling with falling attendance and an aging membership. In addition, there are almost certainly spiritual messages that are useful to the secular as well as to the religious world. Not only are the messages themselves important, but young people's spirituality has also a particular energy, power, and potency that is largely underused.

Arguing the case

Individuals and communities necessarily have a spiritual dimension, and this dimension needs to be supported. With clarity of definition, spirituality can be more easily brought into the field of professional work with young people, and issues can be discussed in straightforward ways.

Lest the work become too overwhelmingly serious, however, let me remind readers of the idea of playfulness in spiritual development. The Mystic, Sufi, and Hasidic traditions, of Christianity, Islam, and Judaism, respectively, have playful and enigmatic stories that invite lighthearted but deeply meaningful exploration. This invitation to play at a deep spiritual level is also found in Zen Buddhism, in which teaching through playful yet profound questions inspires spiritual activity. If we can introduce spirituality to our children and young people in this playful and yet deeply meaningful way, it may inspire and develop their spirituality and profoundly enrich their humanity.

Notes

1. Green, M. (2006). *A journey of discovery: Spirituality in youth work.* Leicester, England: National Youth Agency.

2. See, for example, Aitchinson, J. (2003). *Words in the mind: An introduction to the mental lexicon.* Ames, IA: Wiley-Blackwell.

3. Hull, J. (1999, Autumn). *Youth and Policy.*

4. Green. (2006). P. 31.

5. Board of Education. (1944). *Teachers and youth leaders.* Report of the Committee appointed by the president of the Board of Education to consider the supply, recruitment, and training of teachers and youth leaders ("The McNair Report"). London: HMSO. P. 103.

6. HMSO. (1951). London: Author.

7. Ministry of Education. (1960). The Youth Service in England and Wales ("The Albemarle Report"). London: HMSO. P. 37. See also http://www.infed.org/youthwork/Albemarle_report.htm.

8. See http://www.lifelonglearning.dfee.gov.uk/greenpaper/index.htm.

9. Tagore, R. (1917). *Personality.* New York: Macmillan. Pp. 116–17.

10. National Youth Agency. (2008). *Hear by right.* Available at http://hbr.nya.org.uk/resources/hear_right_book_2008.

MAXINE GREEN *is a consultant to youth-serving agencies through her business I.S.B.D. Ltd., Suffolk, England.*

A youth work practitioner voices her perspectives on spiritual development.

5

Perspectives on spiritual development as part of youth development

Jane Quinn

AS A YOUTH WORK PRACTITIONER, I am intrigued by the long-overdue attention to spiritual development as a component of youth development. At many points along my professional journey, I have pondered my role in this and related areas—often without much support from the youth work community. So it comes as a relief that the Center for Spiritual Development in Childhood and Adolescence is providing much-needed leadership on this topic.

Early in my career, I found myself doing a lot of work in sex education when I was employed in the social work unit of the District of Columbia Health Department. Feeling unprepared for the responsibilities of teaching the facts about human anatomy and reproductive physiology to young people (when no one had explained them very well to me) and providing behavioral guidance (in the absence of clear supervision or organizational frameworks), I did a lot of consulting with experts and reading of professional literature. I was vexed by questions about how to help young people acquire needed knowledge and skills in a value-laden arena without either imposing my values or ignoring the topic of values altogether.

An exhaustive search unearthed an incisive and useful document published by the Sex Information and Education Council of the

WILEY InterScience® DISCOVER SOMETHING GREAT

NEW DIRECTIONS FOR YOUTH DEVELOPMENT, NO. 118, SUMMER 2008 © WILEY PERIODICALS, INC.
Published online in Wiley InterScience (www.interscience.wiley.com) • DOI: 10.1002/yd.257

United States (SIECUS) on moral values and sexuality education. This tiny publication did a good job of explaining the concept of universal moral values—respect, responsibility, honesty, fairness—and the role, even obligation, of secular organizations in fostering these values as part of a comprehensive sexuality education program.

While this explanation satisfied my need at the time, it also left me thirsty for more. I recognized that while the concept of universal moral values is useful, it lacks the kind of depth and nuance needed to address other important developmental questions, particularly the kinds of questions spelled out in the Editors' Notes: How do young people develop their deepest, fundamental commitments? How do they connect to others and the world around them? How do they find their place in their family, community, world, and universe? How do they come to terms with issues of meaning, purpose, and identity beyond themselves?

Several years later, while working on the Carnegie study of American youth organizations (*A Matter of Time: Risk and Opportunity in the Nonschool Hours*), I read a thought-provoking paper that our task force commissioned as part of our study.[1] We asked Kenda Creasy Dean, then a doctoral student at Princeton Theological Seminary, to review the literature on religious youth organizations and analyze the implications of this literature for our national study. One of the key findings of Dean's review was the pronounced effect of religiosity as a protective factor during adolescence. I started wondering: If religious formation and experiences are so effective in protecting young people from harm, what can secular youth organizations learn from our colleagues in religious youth groups? Are there practices and approaches that can translate effectively to nonreligious settings?

I also observed that scores of youth workers cited deeply spiritual motivations for their work—motivation that drew heavily on their understanding of the purpose of human existence, the connections among people, the responsibility of one generation to the next. I was intrigued by their comments, but did not know what to do with them. I left these observations largely untouched in the

Carnegie report, although I knew they were significant—and I hoped I could return to them at some point.

So here I am, fifteen years later, being asked to reflect on the idea of spiritual development as a critical and distinct component of human development. I welcome the opportunity to grapple with the thorny questions embedded in this concept, because I hold out the hope that—finally—many loose ends of my youth-work experience may have an opportunity to become woven together and that I will become a more effective professional in the process.

I am not yet convinced that spiritual development is a separate domain of human development; it may well be a subset of moral development, or it may be an integrating force that works across the other domains. But I am thrilled to see that this area of human experience is generating attention from researchers, practitioners, and young people themselves. The following ideas strike me as particularly compelling:

- *Spiritual development interacts with, yet is distinct from, moral and religious development.* While the lines of demarcation are not totally clear—and in fact these three types of development likely interact regularly—from a conceptual viewpoint, we can think of moral development as encompassing the kinds of universal values outlined twenty-five years ago by SIECUS and others (respect, responsibility, honesty, fairness), religious development as encompassing the beliefs and values of particular faith traditions, and spiritual development as relating to the individual's experience of the self and the outside world.
- *Spiritual development is a core construct of identity formation, one of the central tasks of adolescence.* If we accept that spirit has to do with the animating force that makes us both human and individual, then spiritual development requires that we nurture, feed, and support that animating force. The work of identity formation intensifies during adolescence, and young people feel urgency in creating answers to a host of identity questions: Who am I? and How can I find my place in the world? It makes sense

that youth workers should capitalize on this sense of urgency and provide needed supports and guidance on the spiritual dimensions of youth development (as well as the others).

- *Spiritual development, including spiritual guidance and the development of hope for the future, may have particular salience for vulnerable youth.* I was intrigued to read the emerging evidence suggesting that large numbers of youth in institutional care regard themselves as spiritual or somewhat spiritual. This possibility makes sense when we think about young people as agents of their own development. Francis Ianni and his colleagues, in a landmark study of youth development in diverse communities, found that youth need consistent messages that support their healthy development.[2] It may well be that more vulnerable youth recognize and accept the search for structure that Ianni describes because of the inconsistent or missing supports from other sources (home, school, community).
- *The spiritual dimensions of youth development relate not only to our work with young people but also to our own motivations for engaging in this work.* If we accept (and I do) that spirit encompasses one's sense of purpose and long-term commitments, then the spiritual dimensions of professional youth work seem worthy of greater attention. Could nurturing the spirits of our staff and volunteers result in more effective practice and more successful retention?
- *Youth workers may have an especially important role to play in providing a deliberate counterweight to the rampant materialism in our culture.* Strong forces in our culture have long targeted adolescents as consumers, with great success. Many adolescents have become convinced that "I am what I wear" or "I am what I have." Youth workers can provide useful experiences that help young people move beyond such superficial but attractive constructs. Alternative experiences can help youth create a different inner narrative ("I am a person who likes to help other people"; "I am a poet"; "I am a person who cares about the environment.")
- *Certain types of youth work program content—including the arts, environmental awareness, and service-learning—lend themselves well to spiritual development.* The arts, environment, and service-learning seem to be particularly fertile content areas to foster

positive spiritual development. Visual and performing arts provide important opportunities for self-expression, reflection, and critique; working to improve the environment and other kinds of service-learning naturally raise questions about justice, responsibility, and interconnectedness. By stretching the boundaries of our work a bit, we youth workers can help young people use these experiences to feed their spirits.[3]

- *Basic elements of youth-work practice—including modeling, facilitating authentic conversations, and designing intentional and safe spaces for young people to grapple with important developmental issues—lend themselves well to the work of spiritual growth and understanding.* In youth development, we use a combination of organized experiences and trusting, interpersonal relationships to foster growth in all other areas. Can we not use the same core processes in fostering spiritual development?

The concept of young people's spiritual development is not new—in fact, it has been a lifelong interest of scholars such as Robert Coles. What is new, in my view, is the concept that deliberate attention to spiritual development might be part of secular youth work.

Notes

1. Task Force on Youth Development and Community Programs. (1992). *A matter of time: Risk and opportunity in the nonschool hours.* New York: Carnegie.
2. Ianni, F.A.J. (1990). *The search for structure.* New York: Free Press.
3. See, for example, Coles, R. (1990). *The spiritual life of children.* Boston: Houghton Mifflin.

JANE QUINN *is assistant executive director for Community Schools, Children's Aid Society in New York City.*

We can empower today's youth to explore deep issues in a spirit of openness.

6

KidSpirit magazine: Youth in dialogue about life's big questions

Elizabeth Dabney Hochman

SEVERAL YEARS AGO I was deeply engaged in a career as a performing artist and busy raising two wonderful daughters with my husband, when something about the nexus of motherhood and a spiritual impulse underlying my self-expression as a musician propelled me into a search to address what I see as a black hole in our society.

As I saw my children grow, I felt keenly a strange imbalance facing our children. The vast majority of messages that flash across the billboard-nano-video screens of our young people do not address or even acknowledge a deeper reality or purpose in life. A sense of the underlying importance of seeking one's inner direction is shunted aside and becomes the provenance of discrete communities fractured from the whole.

The implications of this situation are heavy indeed. In a post-9/11 world, we can ignore the walls being erected around disparate communities, or we can attempt to weaken them. We can turn a blind eye to the uncomfortable realities that separate us as a world community, or we can face head-on the new iteration of human discord. For me, a positive way to address this complex situation is through the upcoming generation. If we can empower adolescents to reflect on their sense of inner connection to themselves and the

Published online in Wiley InterScience (www.interscience.wiley.com) • DOI: 10.1002/yd.258

larger community, we will be offering an alternative to at least part of the current reality. For some people, this is too religious, for others, not religious enough. But as defined in the narrow context of our burgeoning magazine, it seems to be working.

KidSpirit magazine was born of a belief that people on the cusp of adulthood need something to counterbalance the many superficial and obfuscating influences bombarding them from our culture at large. I conceived it as a vehicle created by and for kids ages roughly eleven to fifteen to engage each other about values, spirituality, and life's big questions. My goal has been to foster dialogue and understanding among kids of diverse backgrounds and traditions in a nonaffiliated and ad-free forum. Above all, in creating *KidSpirit*, I hoped to empower today's youth to explore deep issues in a spirit of openness. Recently while speaking with nearly two hundred middle schoolers, I had the sense that *KidSpirit* has struck a deep chord. After using the elusive "s" word, I asked them to write what the word *spirit* or *spiritual* means to them. I was beginning to tell the eighth graders that their answers would be anonymous, when two boys shot up out of their seats almost simultaneously and said, "Can I read mine out loud?"

Then one boy, named Nick, walked to the podium, drew himself up, and intoned to his entire grade: "Since I didn't have enough time to define the word *spirit* and *spiritual* in all its uses, I am going to read all of the following: 'Spiritual—the indescribable feeling of connection with everything and nothing. True bliss, sprinkled questions and the journey to find the answer. . . . Flying, and yet a deep connection with the ground. Beauty that is seen with no eyes and felt with no hands. . . . The unlimited question and the undefined answer: The Journey.'"

After a moment of silence, the room erupted in applause, and the other boy, named Mac, quietly sat back down. I went on to read many of the other responses to the group, and then afterward, Mac shyly handed me the following: "Spirit is a compound mixture of all emotions. It is the liquefied love and hatred poured into the bowl of life, along with compassion and carelessness. It is mixed with the spoon of grief, and served into the glass of passion. Spirit is life and life is spiritual."

One student at the school wrote of spirit as “your core self”; another called it “a place inside yourself where you don’t have to be anyone or have an image.” On another paper were the words, “being centered and having a connection with everything around you,” and on another the expansive phrase, “to be free or let go of something.” Yet another described spirit as “an unseeable force that causes energy and happiness in one’s being.” In their totality, these searching comments suggested ample support for this new forum.

In many ways, *KidSpirit* is a reflection of our hybrid society. It is straddling and inclusive of those who identify themselves as going to a church, temple, or synagogue, as well as those who do not. We are not affiliated with any group or organization—a fact that is suspect to some. We dare to put spirituality front and center and in the hands of our young readers and contributors—a radical and worrisome notion to many. But to the children involved in creating each issue, the process is exciting, and to observe and facilitate it is to be filled with wonder.

It has been three years since I first asked myself, *Could this be possible?* More than two years since my older daughter helped me convene an intrepid group of ten- to twelve-year-olds to meet monthly and begin mapping out a spiritual magazine. Throughout this process, I have been amazed by the variety of inner perspectives of our young editorial board. Several are decidedly religious but from different backgrounds. A few are in families in which the parents come from different religious traditions and are practicing one or both faiths, and others are openly agnostic.

On one occasion, two very different boys joined our little band and came in announcing that they were not sure why they were there because they were pretty sure they did not believe in God. It has been more than a year, and they keep coming back in spite of that apparent tension. On the other end of the spectrum, I have several editors who are solidly rooted in a religious tradition and find being invited to explore their own spirituality in this context liberating in a different way.

The primary focus of our editorial board meetings revolves around the kids’ editing each other’s work. Our editors generally express their opinions in a sensitive way. Sometimes, though, even when they make an effort to be aware of the effects of their comments on others, it can be a challenge. Recently a boy had reviewed the movie *Millions* for our issue entitled "Spirit and Materialism." (In the film two young boys, one religious and one not, find a big bag of money and need to figure out what to do with it.) Our reviewer arrived with a rather dismissive, if haughty, assessment of it, and several fellow editors who had seen this movie questioned his approach. He went home with a list of comments that went to the heart of his thesis. Two weeks later, he turned around a draft that had not compromised his view of the movie, but reflected a much deeper sense of its themes than the earlier draft. It was a triumph of the group process as well as the dynamic interaction between the group and his burgeoning inner voice.

While reading the opening article of this volume, I was struck by the ring of truth around Benson and Roehlkepartain's discussion of the word *spiritual.* In my own experience and especially in my role as the founder and editor of *KidSpirit* magazine, I have noted the intense responses that this seemingly innocuous word evinces. To me, the word *spirit,* which encompasses a sense of both the breath of life and the energy of youth, needed to be part of the magazine name. Nonetheless, I was aware that the word has been co-opted by everything from selling Halloween costumes to airline tickets. In everyday use, it is in danger of becoming as empty as the word *nice,* and yet, at least in the context of youth development, it is still quite loaded.

In contemplating Benson and Roehlkepartain's article after my recent school experience, I felt strong anecdotal evidence of what they term "the perceived importance of spirituality" in the students I met. It was also clear that in their definitions, the middle schoolers were pointing to many of the aspects of spirituality offered in the article. The variety and freshness of these manifestos was amazing. However, one additional element was radiating from the many scraps of paper that did not come through strongly in the definitions: awe and passion. In these meetings, my observation was that in this often spiritually underserved age group, the boys and girls I met were almost giddy to be asked to consider what they think about these deep questions. So if there is indeed a sense in which humans spiritually develop, perhaps one marker for this age group is the intensity and fervor with which they express their feelings when they are solicited.

Moreover, it was liberating to be able to invite this exchange in an unaffiliated context. These schoolchildren were encouraged, frankly and anonymously, to bare their true feelings about something many of them may never have been asked to consider before. The still predominant notion among youth workers that spiritual matters are best left to religious institutions may be worth reexamining.

The children I have worked with and met in connection with this project, including those who also have a personal religion at home, seem to find our lack of affiliation to be energizing and inspiring to their inner process. That is not to say that *KidSpirit* magazine is designed in any way to supplant more traditional religious or spiritual avenues; rather, there may be a need for more ways for young people to connect with their sense of spirit, not fewer.

In asking the students to define *spirituality*, my impression was that the open-ended invitation to do so and the thoughtful process that ensued may well be more important to the individuals involved than what their answer happened to be at that moment. It seems that in our culture, this invitation functions in two important ways. First, it suggests to young people that there may be a reality at least as important as the one in which they operate most of the time. Second, by inviting many responses without judgment, we are modeling respect for individual, cultural, and religious differences.

While young people may not be certain of who they are, the path of inner discovery is a worthy one for them to embark on. I believe that in engaging each other on age-old questions, as well as on issues particular to their age, readers of and contributors to *KidSpirit* may have an all-too-rare opportunity to grow holistically—body, mind, emotions, and spirit—and in that process discover their inner wisdom and true voice.

ELIZABETH DABNEY HOCHMAN *is the founder of* KidSpirit *magazine.*

Mentoring has a potentially important role to play in the emotional and spiritual development of today's youth.

7

Youth mentoring and spiritual development

Jean E. Rhodes, Christian S. Chan

RELIGIOUS ORGANIZATIONS OFFER a potentially rich pool of caring adults who are driven by their own spiritual commitments and a strong ethic to serve others.[1] Indeed, more Americans volunteer through religious organizations than through any other venue. Religious organizations account for half of all volunteering, with an estimated 60 percent of the members of religious congregations engaging in volunteerism.[2]

Similarly, a national survey of volunteer mentors indicated that nearly a quarter (24 percent) did so through religious organizations, second only to school. Finally, recent Census Bureau data tracking volunteer trends revealed that 43 percent of American volunteers who engaged in a mentoring relationship did so through religious organizations.[3] It appears, then, that mentoring, especially through faith-based organizations, has a potentially important role to play in the emotional and spiritual development of youth.

A religious congregation represents a rich intergenerational network of parents' friends, extended family members, and spiritual models who can help shape and reinforce not only behavioral and academic outcomes but also spiritual development.[4] Here we use

the term *spirituality* to describe the experience of discovering universal meaning and beliefs and the term *religion* to describe the social, organizational, and practical expression of spirituality.[5]

Mentoring relationships in general and in faith-based organizations can take a wide variety of forms, ranging from the informal connections forged between youth and caring adults to more formal, programmatic ties.[6] Informal mentoring in faith communities often happens through shared activities, such as youth groups, classes, family gatherings, and rituals.

Formal mentoring relationships can arise beyond the bounds of the religious settings through structured mentoring programs. The most prominent faith-based mentoring program in the United States is the Amachi Project. In Amachi (a Nigerian Ibo word meaning "who knows but what God has brought us through this child"), adults are recruited from churches to provide mentoring to children of incarcerated parents. Across the United States, thousands of youth have been mentored through this program,[7] and preliminary studies suggest that participation can lead to improvements in self-efficacy, school performance, and emotional regulation.[8] However, the evaluations have not highlighted the influence of the programs on mentees' spiritual development.

Amachi and other organizations serving children of prisoners have expanded widely in recent years, thanks in part to generous government allocations. Since 2002, the U.S. Congress has authorized millions of dollars to support programs that provide mentors to the children of prisoners. Other federal agencies are also supporting faith-based mentoring through their funding programs. For example, the Juvenile Mentoring Program, which was sponsored through the Office of Juvenile Justice and Delinquency Prevention, awarded 12 percent of its grants to faith-based programs in 2002.[9]

It is important to remain mindful of both the benefits and potential complexities of this relatively new trend in mentoring. One benefit of administering mentoring programs through faith-based organizations is the potential for greater access to children of prisoners and other underrepresented youth, since social policies in general, and mentoring programs in particular, often do not reach the most severely disadvantaged youth. Such organizations have credibility with and access to many disenfranchised families.[10] In addition, mentoring relationships forged through religious organizations could offer some advantages in adolescents' search for meaning, such as reconciliation of their own and their parents' belief systems. Particularly in the light of the associations between religious involvement and positive youth outcomes, mentoring relationships that provide a potential for spiritual and religious development of mentees could serve a protective role.[11]

Some critics, however, have raised concerns over the increasing role of the federal government in supporting faith-based initiatives. Potentially vexing questions concerning the separation of church and state can easily arise.[12] Indeed, the Freedom from Religion Foundation has filed several lawsuits over faith-based mentoring initiatives of the Department of Health and Human Services. One such challenge was to Phoenix-based Mentor Kids USA, which worked only with Christian churchgoing mentors who sign a fundamentalist Christian mission statement. There is also the issue of organizational capacity, for despite their best intentions, religious organizations are not human service agencies. Thus, they are often hard pressed to provide the infrastructure needed to carry out careful screening, training, and ongoing support to volunteer mentors.[13]

Finally, particularly when the mentee is not already a member of a congregation, religiously motivated mentors might feel compelled to advocate particular spiritual paths. Such proselytizing is not supported by empirical evidence and could render the mentoring relationship less effective. Previous research has underscored the importance of nonjudgmental approaches so that the youth can learn to think critically and independently.[14] Few studies, however, have examined the processes that underlie faith-based mentoring programs. Furthermore, it is likely that a more developmentally grounded understanding of spiritual development could give mentors new frameworks for helping their mentees examine this dimension of life without crossing the line into religious proselytizing.

In addition, little is known about the effectiveness of mentoring programs and natural mentoring relationships (in either community or faith-based contexts) on youth's spiritual development or about whether faith-based mentoring programs have any "added value" compared to their secular counterparts. We do know that, as with all other mentoring programs, the success of relationships forged through religious organizations is highly dependent on adherence to empirically supported practices.[15]

For close bonds to arise, mentors and youth need to spend time together on a consistent basis over a significant period of time[16] and engage in positive interactions with each other.[17] Close and enduring ties are fostered when mentors adopt a flexible, youth-centered style in which the young person's interests and preferences are emphasized.[18] To the extent that faith-based mentoring programs can incorporate these lessons, they are well positioned to have a positive impact on our nation's youth.

Notes

1. Maton, K. I., & Sto. Domingo, M. R. (2006). Mobilizing adults for positive youth development: Lessons from religious congregations. In E. G. Clary & J. E. Rhodes (Eds.), *Mobilizing adults for positive youth development.* New York: Springer.

2. Putnam, R. (2000). *Bowling alone: The collapse and revival of American community.* New York: Simon & Schuster.

3. Foster-Bey, J., Dietz, N., & Grimm, R. (2006). *Volunteers mentoring youth: Implications for closing the mentoring gap.* Washington, DC: Corporation for National and Community Service.

4. Regnerus, M. D. (2003). Religion and positive adolescent outcomes: A review of research and theory. *Review of Religious Research, 44,* 394–413.

5. Schwartz, K. D., Bukowski, W. M., & Aoki, W. T. (2006). Mentors, friends, and gurus: Peer and nonparent influences on spiritual development (pp. 310–323). In E. C. Roehlkepartain, P. E. King, L. Wagener, & P. Benson (Eds.), *The handbook of spiritual development in childhood and adolescence.* Thousand Oaks, CA: Sage.

6. Hamilton, S. F., Hamilton, M. A., Hirsch, B. J., Huges, J., King, J., & Maton, K. (2006). Community contexts for mentoring. *Journal of Community Psychology, 34,* 727–746.

7. Goode, W. W., & Smith, T. J. (2005). Building from the ground up: Creating effective programs to mentor children of prisoners (The Amachi Model). *Public/Private Ventures.* Retrieved October 10, 2007, from http://www.ppv.org/ppv/publications/assets/185_publication.pdf.

8. Jucovy, L. (2003). Mentoring children of prisoners in Philadelphia. *Public/Private Ventures.* Retrieved October 10, 2007, from http://www.ppv.org/ppv/publications/assets/21_publication.pdf.

9. Clarke, S., Forbush, J., & Henderson, J. (2003). *Faith-based mentoring: A preventive strategy for at-risk youth.* Paper presented at the Fourteenth National Conference on Child Abuse and Neglect.

10. Dionne, E.J., & DiIlulio, J. J., Jr. (Eds.). (2000). *What's God got to do with the American experiment?* Washington, DC: Brookings Institution.

11. Regnerus. (2003).

12. Branch, A. Y. (2002). *Faith and action: Implementation of the National Faith-Based Initiative for High Risk Youth.* Philadelphia: Public/Private Ventures; Maton, K. I., Sto. Domingo, M. R., & King, J. (2005). Faith-based organizations. In D. L. DuBois & M. Karcher (Eds.), *Handbook of youth mentoring* (pp. 276–391). Thousand Oaks, CA: Sage.

13. Maton et al. (2005).

14. Styles, M., & Morrow, K. (1992). *Understanding how youth and elders form relationships: A study of four linking lifetimes programs.* Philadelphia: Public/Private Ventures.

15. DuBois, D. L., Holloway, B. E., Valentine, J. C., & Cooper, H. (2002). Effectiveness of mentoring programs: A meta-analytical review. *American Journal of Community Psychology, 30,* 157–197.

16. Grossman, J., & Rhodes, J. (2002). The test of time: Predictors and effects of duration in youth mentoring relationships. *American Journal of Community Psychology, 30*(2), 199–219.

17. Rhodes, J. E., & DuBois, D. L. (2006). Understanding and facilitating the youth mentoring movement. *Social Policy Report, 20*(3), 3–23.

18. Morrow, K. V., & Styles, M. B. (1995). *Building relationships with youth in program settings: A study of BigBrothers/BigSisters.* Philadelphia: Public/Private Ventures; Styles and Morrow (1992); Karcher, M. J. (2005). The effects of school-based developmental mentoring and mentors' attendance on mentees' self-esteem, behavior, and connectedness. *Psychology in the Schools, 42,* 65–77.

JEAN E. RHODES *is a professor of psychology at the University of Massachusetts, Boston.*

CHRISTIAN S. CHAN *is a doctoral student at the University of Massachusetts, Boston.*

Service-learning is an important, effective vehicle to encourage the spiritual development of young people.

8

The spiritual nature of service-learning

Liane J. Louie-Badua, Maura Wolf

IMAGINE A FOURTH-GRADE student working in a community garden, growing tomatoes for the local farmers' market. Working side by side with his classmates, he is putting his hands in the dirt and participating in the organic process of seeding the earth, watering new life, trusting growth, and, later, celebrating the harvest. Such an experience is a metaphor for living he is likely not to understand yet, but also a practical experience that may broaden his sense of interconnectedness to others and the environment—and, many would argue, a spiritual process that expands his world in ways that may lead to spiritual growth and personal transformation.

Research has clearly indicated that engaging in service substantially enhances a student's academic achievement, civic engagement, and life skills development in meaningful ways. Service-learning is also an important and effective vehicle to encourage the spiritual development of young people.

In secular education, with a society that has become diverse and pluralistic, the spiritual development of young people has been neglected. We define *spirituality* broadly as one's subjective awareness and internal values, with the ability to explore the meaning and purpose of our lives. The Shinnyo-en Foundation, established in 1994 by a lay Buddhist order, has supported service-learning

Published online in Wiley InterScience (www.interscience.wiley.com) • DOI: 10.1002/yd.260

programs with and without a spiritual component, and has found that programs that incorporate spiritual exploration and dialogue can deepen the experience for young people.

The foundation is committed to supporting and advocating the spiritual growth of young people in secular education as a part of holistic development. Through our past twelve years of grant making, we have discovered three important and related spiritual dimensions of service-learning:

- Experiencing a sense of interconnectedness with others and the environment
- Opening your heart to those around you, including those you have previously thought to be "other"
- Reflecting that expands self-inquiry and knowledge about one's background, values, purpose, and meaning

Experiencing a sense of interconnectedness

Spiritual endeavors often call us into a place of question rather than answer: Why? Why now? What is my place in the world? How do I connect to my ancestors and community? How do I make meaning of what is happening here? For young people, these questions are pressing and uncomfortable. Service-learning can foster the context for spiritual growth and development by encouraging group connection. Service experiences demonstrate a cooperative rather than competitive experience and promote skills associated with teamwork and community involvement.[1] Service also encourages the sense of belonging and connection to the larger world.

Opening your heart

Love exists as a central theme in all major religions and philosophies, and we have found that creating the environment for an open heart is a key factor in cultivating love, empathy, and compassion. To open your heart means to be open to others around you, to be open to differences, to be open to feelings you may have never experienced before.

Service-learning encourages intentional learning communities in which teachers move away from theoretical teaching to experiencing learning with their students. The foundation calls this "reciprocity of service," which means that both the giver and the receiver of the service are experiencing positive benefits from the service relationship. Thus, an open heart encourages a young person to feel connected to others and to experience compassion for another person. Many young people in programs we have supported report a deeper understanding of human connectedness and gratitude when reflecting their service actions.

Reflecting that expands self-inquiry and knowledge

Through service-learning, student and teacher venture into the larger community to obtain a hands-on, experiential understanding of a topic (for example, in studying homelessness, the student might volunteer at a homeless shelter) and return to the classroom for individual and group-directed reflection on the topic.

This process allows deeper meaning by placing the overall experience in the context of the larger society. Through guided reflection, the student begins to understand the meaning of homelessness for herself, reflects on the stereotypes or biases she carries, and starts to think about solutions and interconnections. Through the power of reflection, the student is able to gain meaning and integration of the issue that was both studied and practiced.

Alexander Astin spoke of the importance of spirituality as deserving a central place in liberal education, as it encourages reflection on two important questions: "Who am I?" and, "How can we know others if we do not know ourselves?" He makes a strong case for students knowing their interior life versus the outer.[2] Service-learning can encourage exploration of these critical questions.

The action of service encourages a deeper and authentic experience to the connection between our inner lives and outer actions.[3] Strain argues that service-learning experiences can contribute to transformational learning, defined as "an alteration of our frame of reference," and represents the change of the structure of one's assumptions and expectations through filtered impressions.[4] A student who ventures outside into the world begins to see diverse experiences that may affirm or contradict initial impressions and perceptions. Transformational learning can be an opportunity for both spiritual and social transformation.

Strain states that the potential for transformation is built on critical reflection and caring relationships. Through profound transformative experiences, the student gains the potential for a spiritual awakening to new understandings.[5]

Kent Koth argues for a powerful spiritual reflection model that combines the spiritual element of the campus ministry model with the reflective practice of the experiential learning model.[6] This model engages students in service activities and then in reflection on social issues and personal spirituality. Reflection that delves into personal purpose, values, and meaning can create the opportunity for a person to touch on her or his purpose and calling.

Eyler and Giles believe that service-learning outcomes lead to increased tolerance for diversity, greater self-knowledge and spiritual growth, and a greater sense of community connectedness.[7] Spirituality, which is subjective to an individual, can also foster a lifetime commitment to serve. Through repeated cycles of spiritual reflection and service, this interconnected process of personal and community discovery is created. The community, an interrelated part of the process, supports the individual to deepen his or her understanding of service, purpose, and meaning.

The spiritual dimensions of a fourth grader's experience of service in a community garden might include connecting with the earth as he digs, with the hope he holds for the future harvest, or working alongside peers he does not yet know well. These spiritual dimensions, whether we recognize them or not, can bring a powerful added value to the service experience. Service-learning can certainly change a person's life; service-learning with attention to the subjective awareness of those spiritual factors can also bring a lifetime commitment to serve.

Notes

1. Eyler, J., & Giles, D. E. (1999). *Where's the learning in service-learning?* San Francisco, Jossey-Bass.
2. Astin, W. A. (2004). Why spirituality deserves a central place in liberal education. *Liberal Education, 90*(2), 34–41.
3. Astin. (2004).
4. Strain, C. R. (2006). Moving like a starfish: Beyond a unilinear model of student transformation in service learning classes. *Journal of College and Character, 8*(1), 1–12.
5. Koth, K. (2004). *Deepening the commitment to serve: Spiritual reflections in service-learning.* Unpublished master's thesis, University of California, Berkeley.
6. Koth, K. (2003). Deepening the commitment to serve. *About Campus, 7*(5), 2–7.
7. Eyler & Giles. (1999).

LIANE J. LOUIE-BADUA *is the progam officer of the Shinnyo-en Foundation in San Francisco.*

MAURA WOLF *is a consultant to the Shinnyo-en Foundation in San Francisco.*

Rites of passage include the intentional design of opportunities for children to experience wonder and awe.

9

Coming of age and awakening to spiritual consciousness through rites of passage

David G. Blumenkrantz, Kathryn L. Hong

ALL CHILDREN HAVE an innate need to engage in experiences that precipitate a spiritual awakening. Parents and community institutions (school, youth and family agencies, civic and faith organizations, government, and others) need to take on roles and responsibilities that support this awakening.

Pathways to spirit

Rites of passage have been a human pathway to such spiritual consciousness for more than ten thousand years. Yet in contemporary American communities, few socially sanctioned, community-based rites of passage exist with enough breadth and depth to have an impact on an individual's identity and sense of community. The void created by this lack of guidance toward deeper meaning during

coming of age can contribute to such problems as cynicism, materialism, substance use, and violence.

The Rite of Passage Experience

The Rite of Passage Experience (ROPE) is a three-phase, six-year youth and community development process that integrates ancient symbols and contemporary youth and community development strategies to create a powerful coming-of-age process for children within the entire community.

Although ROPE has prescribed elements, the elements work together more as a structure for fostering a collaborative process within a community. Thus, its most distinguishing feature is not its program elements but its ability to mobilize a community, within a common language and shared emotional experience, to create and sustain a community-focused rite-of-passage initiative.

There are three phases to a ROPE. Phase I (the transition from primary to secondary school) focuses community, parent, student, and school attention on children's separation from elementary school, the beginning of their separation from parents, and the importance of these transitions. A core curriculum of life skills prepares students for the complex challenges ahead. An initial orientation fosters the opportunity for awakening to spirit.

Phase II (middle school) intentionally creates ways of connecting youth to the concepts of transformation and transcendence through play by systematically guiding youth into positive leisure-time activities. When children find their bliss, their spark, this experience can serve as a powerful protective factor and promote health for their entire lifetime.

Phase III (high school) systematically guides youth into community service. High school students serve as ROPE facilitators in phase I and mentors for younger students, guiding middle school students into positive leisure-time activities and helping them make a safe transition to high school.

A sense of awe and wonder

A key ingredient in ROPE is the design of intentional opportunities for children to experience a sense of wonder, awe, and connection to things perceived to be greater than themselves in ways that contribute to their spiritual development.

In phase I, an initiation event is central. Parents and students are "summoned" to an important evening meeting by the principal of their school, the town's mayor, or another identified community leader. The children are separated from their parents and join in an emotionally engaging experience that awakens them to their impending transition to adulthood, promotes a sense of connection and wonder, and introduces the expectations of their community. Parents are engaged in a presentation about the challenges of this coming-of-age transition, the function of the Rite of Passage Experience, and their roles and responsibilities within the process.

In one dramatic initiation event, a faith community awakened their eleven- and twelve-year-old children from their beds on a Saturday night. Community elders accompanied them to a forest, where they sat around a campfire talking about coming of age, the ROPE process, and the community's expectation for their transformation and transition to adulthood. The children began a process of reflection and dialogue and engaged in individual and group problem-solving challenges. At sunrise the initiates and elders returned to their faith community's house of worship, where their parents and the congregation greeted them, acknowledged the beginning of their transformation to adulthood, and conducted a sunrise worship service.

In this way, the transformation and transcendence of the children begins and is honored and celebrated by the children's community. A quotation from Antoine de Saint-Exupéry indicates something of the way the process works: "If you want to build a ship, don't drum up people together to collect wood and don't assign them tasks and work, but rather teach them to long for the endless immensity of the sea.[1]"

Note

1. de Saint-Exupéry, A. http://thinkexist.com/quotation/if_you_want_to_build_a_ship-don-t_drum_up_people/170927.html.

DAVID G. BLUMENKRANTZ *is the founder and executive director of the Center for the Advancement of Youth, Family and Community Services in Glastonbury, Connecticut, and co-creator of ROPE.*

KATHRYN L. HONG *is senior projects manager of Search Institute, Minneapolis, Minnesota.*

How can contemplative education assist in helping young people develop concentration, awareness, and compassion?

10

Contemplative education and youth development

Patricia A. Jennings

AFTER MORE THAN forty years of growing interest, regular contemplative practice has become a more central part of the American lifestyle. In 1998, the General Social Survey found that 32.7 percent of adults surveyed reported meditating once a week or more, and a burgeoning industry of wellness practitioners promotes meditative practices as a means of improving health and general well-being.[1] As a result of this interest, a rapidly growing international movement aims to promote well-being among children and youth through contemplative education.[2]

Contemplation and spiritual development

With roots in ancient religious and spiritual traditions, contemplative practices developed across human history to promote the three primary dimensions of spiritual development outlined by Benson and Roehlkepartain in the lead article in this volume: belonging and connecting, awareness and awakening, and a way of living. Included are practices to promote love, compassion, and

connection; to promote powers of concentration and enhanced awareness of self and other; and to bring awareness into the activities of daily living to promote a wholesome lifestyle. Contemplative practices can involve sitting quietly (such as in meditation), movement (such as yoga and tai chi), and the contemplation of nature or the arts,[3] and they can be found in both the religious and secular realms.[4]

Contemplation as spiritual practice may be described as a developmental resource—the engine that drives spiritual development—because it promotes access to direct spiritual experience. Over time the practitioner develops a contemplative capacity—the ability to access and maintain contemplative awareness during contemplative practice and eventually within the activities of daily life.[5]

Evidence that children spontaneously experience contemplative states beginning in early childhood suggests that contemplation is a natural human capacity that can be nurtured through encouragement and practice.[6] It also supports the argument that spiritual development is an intrinsic part of the human life span developmental process that begins early in life.[7]

Given the evidence that contemplative practices support valued developmental outcomes in adulthood, including spiritual development and improved attention, reduced stress, and increased prosocial responding, it is reasonable to assume that contemplation may promote equally valuable outcomes among children and youth.[8] However, children are not just small adults; a careful examination of how contemplative practices may be introduced to meet developmental needs with attention to multiple domains (cognitive, biological, socioemotional, and spiritual) across each stage is required. To date, the empirical evidence to inform practice is extremely limited.

A promising possibility is that well-designed contemplative interventions may promote the executive functions and self-regulatory capabilities found to be important prerequisites for children's learning and caring for others. Contemplative practices may also support children's quest for meaning and promote positive experiences of wonder and awe that motivate learning.

Contemplative education

As the number of contemplative practitioners grows, more teachers, parents, and school administrators are exploring ways to introduce contemplation in school settings to support mindful learning. Contemplative education refers more to how one learns than what one learns. In some cases it refers to how one unlearns unhealthy habitual patterns. Roeser and Peck define contemplative education as "a set of pedagogical practices that have as their aim personal and social transformation through the cultivation of conscious and willful awareness." These practices help young people develop the self-awareness to recognize mental and behavioral habits and learn ways to transcend habitual patterns "in favor of more mindful and willful forms of living, learning, and relating to others."[9]

Contemplation also may enhance learning by offering alternative ways of knowing that complement the rational and sensory. Hart argues that contemplative knowing is an important missing link that connects students to universally shared human values and an exploration of life's meaning.[10]

Contemplative education has its roots in alternative educational methodologies, particularly in the United States, where the concern for division of church and state has been viewed as an obstacle to bringing contemplative education into mainstream public educational settings. The clear articulation of spiritual development as an essential human process outside the context of religion may alleviate this concern.

Educational reformers such as Maria Montessori and Rudolf Steiner recognized the spiritual life and development of the child and designed methods of teaching to nurture this capacity from infancy through adolescence. In line with Montessori[11] and Steiner,[12] some argue that the introduction of contemplative practices to children should follow and nurture the child's innate inclinations by providing opportunities for naturally occurring contemplation and infusing the curriculum with a contemplative orientation.[13] Both of these educational philosophies offer examples of developmentally appropriate contemplative curriculum involving movement, the arts, the study of nature, and practicing silence.

Montessori and Steiner point to the importance of the adult's contemplative capacity in supporting children's development. Parents and teachers with strong contemplative capacities can tune into the child's natural inclination toward the contemplative and guide and nurture it by modeling contemplative behavior in everyday life. Such adults find skillful ways to weave the contemplative into their ordinary lessons rather than imposing a contemplative activity out of the context of the daily classroom rhythm.

Contemplation may be a natural human capacity that begins early in life and can be nurtured through practice. It provides the practitioner an opportunity to directly experience the spiritual by promoting belonging and connecting, awareness, and a wholesome way of living. Contemplative education offers alternative ways of knowing and the potential for more mindful learning. However, developmental needs and capacities should be carefully considered when introducing contemplative practices to children and youth.

Notes

1. Abeles, R., Ellison, C., George, L., Idler, E., Krause, N., Levin, J., et al. (1999). *Multiple dimensions of spiritual experience.* Kalamazoo, MI: Fetzer Institute.
2. Garrison Institute. (2005). *Contemplation and education: A survey of programs using contemplative techniques in K-12 educational settings: A mapping report.* Garrison, NY: Garrison Institute.
3. Caranfa, A. (2006). Voices of silence in pedagogy: Art, writing and self-encounter. *Journal of Philosophy of Education, 40,* 85–103.
4. Kesson, K., Traugh, C., & Perez, F. (2006). Descriptive inquiry as contemplative practice. *Teachers College Record, 108,* 1862–1880.
5. Trungpa, C. (1972). *Meditation in action.* Boston: Shambhala Press.
6. Hart, T. (2003). *The secret spiritual world of children.* Novato, CA: New World Library; Hart, T. (2004). The mystical child: Glimpsing the spiritual world of children. *Encounter: Education for Meaning and Social Justice, 17,* 38–49.
7. For example, Benson, P. L., Roehlkepartain, E. C., & Rude, S. P. (2003). Spiritual development in childhood and adolescence: Toward a field of inquiry. *Applied Developmental Science,* 7, 204–212; Kline, K. K. (2008). *Authoritative communities: The scientific case for nurturing the whole child.* New York: Springer; Roehlkepartain, E. C., King, P. E., Wagener, L. M., & Benson, P. L. (2006).

The handbook of spiritual development in childhood and adolescence. Thousand Oaks, CA: Sage.

8. Murphy, M., & Donovan, S. (1999). *The physical and psychological effects of meditation: A review of contemporary research with a comprehensive bibliography, 1931–1996.* Sausalito, CA: Institute of Noetic Sciences.

9. Roeser, R. W., & Peck, S. C. (in press). An education in awareness: Human identity in contemplative perspective. *Educational Psychologist.*

10. Hart, T. (2002). Opening the contemplative mind in the classroom. *Journal of Transformative Education, 2,* 28–46.

11. Montessori, M. (1936). *The secret of childhood.* New York: Frederick A. Stokes.

12. Steiner, R. (1907). *The education of the child.* Great Barrington, MA: Anthroposophic Press.

13. Wolf, A. D. (1996). *Nurturing the spirit in non-sectarian classrooms.* Hollidaysburg, PA: Parent Child Press.

PATRICIA A. JENNINGS *is the director of the Initiative on Contemplation and Education at the Garrison Institute and holds a faculty position in Child and Adolescent Development at San Francisco State University.*

The spiritual growth of young people has been a core focus in camp settings for almost 150 years.

11

Spiritual development and camp experiences

Karla A. Henderson, M. Deborah Bialeschki

CAMP EXPERIENCES HAVE been and will continue to be promising practices in nurturing spiritual development. The physical, mental, social, and spiritual growth of campers has been at the core of camps for almost 150 years. Beautiful natural settings, opportunities for bonding with others, and rituals associated with camp experiences provide a significant backdrop for spiritual growth in young people.

The earliest researchers studying organized camping argued that character development had components of spirituality.[1] Camping, woodcraft, and Indian lore were seen as effective ways of interesting children in the "spiritual message of the YMCA."[2] Chenery stated that "we in camping have an opportunity and responsibility to become sanctuaries for the nurturance of spiritual growth and empowerment."[3]

As Benson and Roehlkepartain noted in the opening article in this volume, the American Camp Association (ACA) undertook a national outcomes study in 2001–2002 with spiritual development as one of ten potential constructs associated with camp.[4] The results for spiritual development measured by both campers (eight to seventeen years old) and parents showed significant positive

WILEY InterScience® DISCOVER SOMETHING GREAT

Published online in Wiley InterScience (www.interscience.wiley.com) • DOI: 10.1002/yd.263

change, whether associated with religiously affiliated camps or another sponsorship (that is, independent for-profit, independent nonprofit, and agency camps).

Several other studies have examined dimensions of spirituality and religiosity in camp. Clampit found references to nature being used as a sacred symbol at camp dating back to a 1915 camp newspaper.[5] Sweatman and Heintzman discovered that the perceived impact of outdoor residential camp experiences associated with spirituality included the actual camp setting, time alone, social opportunities, and positive feelings.[6] Yust's interviews with campers at Christian camps in Indiana showed that campers valued the sense of social community more than spiritual formation.[7]

Camp experiences offer the potential for spiritual development, but often in an implicit and tangential way. Chenery emphasized that while experiential spontaneous spiritual growth can occur in camps, "at least some of the camp's teaching of spiritual centering must be explicit, overt, concrete, and planned."[8] The camp environment with its traditions and rituals that encourage a "quieting of the mind" can cultivate an experience of connection with God, higher powers, the natural world, or other living beings. McDonald and Schreyer suggested that rituals, communion with God or nature, music, and contemplation may be precursors to religious and spiritual experiences.[9] Rather than spiritual development being the engine that propels the search for connectedness, meaning, purpose, and contribution, a camp experience based on positive youth development goals offers youth a path to spiritual development.

The challenge to camp professionals as well as other youth workers is to consider how spiritual growth can be articulated and measured. In ACA's study of outcomes, not only was defining spirituality difficult but trying to operationalize the construct for data collection was complicated.[10] For example, was "higher power" understood in the same way as "God"? How does spirituality differ from religiosity? These two concepts may not be the same, so more research is necessary to explore their meaning in camps.

The critical theoretical issues that Benson and Roehlkepartain raised are pertinent for camp experiences. Issues of how spirituality might develop during a camp session require greater exploration, as does the way spiritual growth might be experienced by campers who return to camp year after year. The transcendental nature of the outdoors may provide a crucial foundation for spiritual development in some young people. The connections to others through camp and camp rituals provide another area for exploration that relates to a sense of community and personal identity. The question raised about spirituality as an individual or collective phenomenon suggests that camp embodies both, but the mechanisms are not clear. As noted, spirituality is a cognitive and affective mixture. While religiously affiliated camps may address the cognitive dimensions more so than other camps, affective dimensions are omnipresent in most camps.

Camp experiences can clearly contribute to this ongoing dialogue and provide a context for addressing spirituality, whether explicitly or implicitly. The camp context is unique because of the combination of the outdoor natural world and group living. With the important role that nature plays in individuals' understanding of spirituality, the camp experience may provide many youth with a context for spiritual development unavailable to them in other settings.

Notes

1. Dimock, H. S., & Hendry, C. E. (1929). *Camping and character: A camp experiment in character education.* New York: Association Press.

2. Van Slyck, A. A. (2006). *A manufactured wilderness: Summer camps and the shaping of American youth, 1890–1960.* Minneapolis: University of Minnesota Press. P. 111.

3. Chenery, M. F. (1984). Nurturing the human spirit in camping. *Camping Magazine,* 57(1), 22.

4. American Camp Association. (2005). *Directions: Youth development outcomes of the camp experience.* Martinsville, IN: Author.

5. Clampit, M. K. (1970). Nature as a sacred symbol in religiously oriented summer camps. *Journal for the Scientific Study of Religion,* 9(2), 151–152.

6. Sweatman, M. M., & Heintzman, P. (2004). The perceived impact of outdoor residential camp experience on the spirituality of youth. *World Leisure Journal,* 46(1), 23–31.

7. Yust, K. (2006). Creating an idyllic world for children's spiritual formation. *International Journal of Children's Spirituality,* 11(1), 177–188.

8. Chenery. (1984), P. 24.
9. McDonald, B. L., & Schreyer, R. (1991). Spiritual benefits of leisure participation and leisure settings. In B. L. Driver, P. J. Brown, & G. L. Peterson (Eds.), *Benefits of leisure* (pp. 179–184). State College, PA: Venture Publishing.
10. Henderson, K. A., Thurber, C. A., Whitaker, L. S., Bialeschki, M. D., & Scanlin, M. (2006). Development and application of a camper growth index for youth. *Journal of Experiential Education, 29*(1), 1–17.

KARLA A. HENDERSON *is on the faculty in the Department of Parks, Recreation and Tourism Management, North Carolina State University.*

M. DEBORAH BIALESCHKI *is senior researcher for the American Camp Association.*

To be competent practitioners in spiritual development, youth workers must begin with their own experiences.

12

Spiritual development in youth worker preparation: A matter of resolve

Elisabeth M. Kimball

THE ISSUE TODAY is not how to integrate spiritual development into youth worker preparation; it is whether we have the resolve to do so. Once an organization is confident that attentiveness to spiritual development has the potential to enrich and improve youth work practice, equipping workers with the necessary capacities and skills is the easier part.

The growing research on spiritual development, new forms and complexities of religious pluralism,[1] and evidence of growing interest in spirituality in popular culture[2] make compelling reasons to reexamine assumptions that maintained distinctions between religious and secular youth work in the late twentieth century. As Tacey puts it, "The spiritual life is no longer a specialist concern, confined to the interests of a religious group."[3] Outdated assumptions conflate spiritual development with religious formation and have maintained a chasm between faith-based and secular youth work.

Today young people form identities, make meaning, and discern life's purpose in neighborhoods, schools, parks, prisons, malls, and

NEW DIRECTIONS FOR YOUTH DEVELOPMENT, NO. 118, SUMMER 2008 © WILEY PERIODICALS, INC.
Published online in Wiley InterScience (www.interscience.wiley.com) • DOI: 10.1002/yd.264

workplaces, and on buses and social networking Web sites, all filled with diverse religious views and spiritual practices. Spiritual development can no longer be tidily or naively confined to the family and religious institutions.

Doctrinal distinctions between *secular* and *sacred,* reinforced in the United States by (mis)interpretations of the First Amendment religion clauses, have led youth workers to a fearful avoidance of all things religious and spiritual in other than faith-based organizations. The rise of evangelical Christianity in the United States in the 1980s, with its powerful political infrastructure and its passion for youth ministry, reinforced the idea of equating spirituality in youth work with proselytizing. Today residual fear is regularly aggravated by news of growing global fundamentalism in Islam, Judaism, and Christianity.

It takes courage for the leadership of a youth-serving agency or program to recognize that spirituality is a natural dimension of youth development, distinct from religiosity. Once such resolve is demonstrated, youth workers can be equipped with the capacity for critical spirituality (awareness of and attentiveness to diverse experiences of spirituality) and prepared to nurture healthy spiritual development in others.[4]

One model for such preparation comes from a popular course, Young People's Spirituality and Youth Work, that has been taught for four years at the University of Minnesota to graduate and undergraduate youth students:

1. Begin with a self-selected group. Do not impose conversation about spirituality. Look for opportunities to cultivate organic interest.
2. Provide a safe, structured environment for youth workers to reflect on and articulate their own spiritual autobiographies, however they define them.
3. Share the autobiographies. Notice the vocabulary people use. Identify common domains and moments of spiritual experience (such as crisis or death of a loved one or experiences of nature).

4. Build a common lexicon. Establish working definitions of words embedded in the group members' spiritual and religious landscapes.
5. Wrestle with the relationship between religion and spirituality. Do not force consensus; invite expanded awareness. Review relevant legal protections such as the First Amendment to the U.S. Constitution.[5]
6. Introduce available discipline- or profession-specific literature on spirituality.[6] Integrate personal experience to establish context-appropriate definitions of spirituality.
7. Review human development theory, and locate the youth workers' definitions of spirituality as a dimension of potential development.
8. Put theory into practice. As a group discuss the following:
   - If healthy spiritual development, as now defined, is important in the lives of young people, what can youth workers do to enhance and facilitate such awareness and growth?
   - How can they establish a climate and practices that respect and nurture spiritual development?
   - What resources do they need?
   - What resistance do they anticipate?

If we want youth workers who are competent practitioners in the domain of spiritual development, we must begin with their own experiences of spirituality and religion. The capacity to recognize and nurture the spiritual development of others grows with attentiveness to one's own spiritual journey.

Once introduced, spiritual development in youth worker preparation is an ongoing reflexive process. It simultaneously equips individuals to be more attentive to and confident about spiritual dimensions of everyday life and professional practice, while it transforms the environment in which their work is conducted. Lerner calls this "emancipatory spirituality" with the power to construct healthy communities.[7] Spiritual development training will always require moral vigilance—acknowledgment of the cultural, political, and linguistic contexts in which it is taking place, and deep respect for each person's story. It is ultimately about creating space in which mystery and human potential meet.

Notes

1. Eck, D. (2001). *A new religious America: How a "Christian country" has become the world's most religiously diverse nation.* New York: HarperCollins; Wuthnow, R. (2005). *America and the challenges of religious diversity.* Princeton, NJ: Princeton University Press.

2. Forbes, B. D., & Mahan, J. H. (2005). *Religion and popular culture in America.* Berkeley: University of California Press.

3. Tacey, D. (2004). *The spirituality revolution: The emergence of contemporary spirituality.* New York: Routledge.

4. Bagwell, T. (2003). Defining spirituality in public higher education: A response to R. J. Nash from a spiritually engaged atheist. *Religion and Education, 30*(2). Retrieved May 13, 2008, from http://www.uni.edu/coe/jrae/Fall%202003/Bagwell%20Excerpt%20Fa%2003.htm.

5. See First Amendment Center, www.firstamendmentcenter.org.

6. For example, in the field of education, see Crawford, M., & Rossiter, G. (2006). *Reasons for living: Education and young people's search for meaning, identity and spirituality. A handbook.* Camberwell, Victoria, Australia: ACER Press; Lantieri, L. (Ed.). (2001). *Schools with spirit: Nurturing the inner lives of children and teachers.* Boston: Beacon. In the field of social work, see Canda, E., & Furman, L. (1999). *Spiritual diversity in social work practice: The heart of helping.* New York: Free Press.

7. Lerner, M. (2000). *Spirit matters.* Charlottesville, VA: Hampton Roads Publishing.

ELISABETH M. KIMBALL *is a lecturer in youth studies at the University of Minnesota and a consultant to the Center for Spiritual Development in Childhood and Adolescence, Search Institute, Minneapolis, Minnesota.*

Spiritual concepts can play a unique role in addressing key issues for vulnerable youth.

13

Spiritual development with marginalized youth: A status report

Melanie Wilson, Kristal S. Nicholson

IN THE PAST SEVERAL years, social service agencies that work with marginalized youth have reported increased interest in using spiritual activities as one tool in a more standard array of therapeutic interventions. ("Marginalized youth" are defined here as adolescents or young adults who are in foster care, homeless, in family crisis, involved with the juvenile justice system, or in treatment for mild to moderate mental or behavioral health issues.) Where it has occurred, the use of spirituality in such settings tends to reflect the agencies' belief that spiritual concepts have a unique role to play in addressing issues of key importance to their clients: belonging, community, forgiveness, meaning, purpose, and acknowledgment of a universal moral or ethical code.

A 2002 study asked social service providers about the number and kinds of spiritually oriented activities they used in their work with adolescents.[1] Of the 191 agencies interviewed, more than half reported using one or more nonreligious spiritual activities with their clients, and over a third offered religious activities. A majority of providers expressed interest in developing or expanding their

WILEY InterScience® DISCOVER SOMETHING GREAT

Published online in Wiley InterScience (www.interscience.wiley.com) • DOI: 10.1002/yd.265

spiritual programming, with secular providers expressing particular enthusiasm for introducing meditative or "mindfulness" practices.

Secular spiritual practices

Among the most popular such practices in social service settings are meditation, yoga, and guided visualization, which are meant to promote a sense of calm, connectedness, and even transcendence. Musical and artistic expression, traditional martial arts, and rites-of-passage programs are also common. Usually such activities are voluntary and performed in group settings.

Due to the difficulty of obtaining large sample sizes, relatively few rigorous outcome evaluations have been conducted on the impact of these activities on troubled youth. Yet emerging research suggests that mindfulness practices are promising tools in reducing depression, anxiety, anger, and other problems typical in adolescent clients.[2] Because of these perceived benefits, several national and regional organizations have formed in the past decade to teach mindfulness techniques to at-risk youth, particularly in the juvenile justice system.

Religious involvement

The influence of religion on youth has been widely researched. Although the precise mechanisms are unclear, religiosity and active religious participation are well-documented protective factors for young people, delaying or reducing the likelihood of teen pregnancy, substance abuse, delinquency, and other destructive behaviors. Social scientists have suggested that involvement in organized religion provides youth with opportunities to acquire cross-generational connections, leadership skills, and "cultural capital."[3]

Religious activities, when they are offered in agency settings, include religious education classes, pastoral counseling, worship services, and faith-motivated community service projects.

Some characteristics of positive spiritual programming for youth in agency settings (religious and secular) have been proposed.[4] Agencies developing such programs for adolescent clients should consider spiritual exploration and growth a core part of treatment, involve youth as decision makers, allow youth to participate in spiritual programming as much or as little as they wish, and match spiritual programming to youth's cultural backgrounds.

Obstacles to development of spiritual programming

Ongoing debate over the definition of spirituality, and uncertainties about the appropriateness and legal permissibility of certain spiritual activities, are serious obstacles to the development of this area of practice.

Efforts to clarify the appropriate uses of spirituality in child welfare practice are under way. In one 2005 initiative, the National Resource Center for Youth Services developed and implemented a training curriculum, Integrating Spirituality with Youth Work. The curriculum, used to train state child welfare workers, is meant to help social service providers see spirituality as a potential missing link in the healing process for marginalized youth and to underscore the relationship of spirituality to permanency.[5] As part of the curriculum, providers are asked to examine their own spiritual beliefs and values and to ask themselves whether personal biases for or against spirituality are interfering with their ethical commitment to their young clients. The training introduces tools to enhance current treatment interventions and spiritual development of youth and offers professionals the opportunity to receive training in spirituality and religious culture to better address adolescents' development needs in context.

Other attempts to bolster and legitimize spiritual programming for marginalized youth can be found in relatively new college-level courses that address the integration of spirituality into clinical practice (see the article by Elisabeth M. Kimball in this volume); increased interest among academic and practitioners in research on spirituality; and new partnerships, encouraged in the past decade by the federal government, between faith-based and secular groups that work with young people.

As momentum builds toward adoption of spiritual practice in agency settings, questions about the precise benefits of specific activities, and the ongoing tension regarding appropriateness, will become even more urgent. Organized efforts must be made to resolve these questions if spiritual programming for vulnerable youth is to continue to develop.

Notes

1. Wilson, M. (2002). *Practice unbound: A study of secular spiritual and religious activities in work with adolescents.* Boxborough, MA: New England Network for Child, Youth and Family Services.

2. Wilson. (2002).

3. Larson, D., & Johnson, B. (1998). *Religion: The forgotten factor in cutting youth crime and saving at-risk urban youth.* Manhattan Institute for Policy Research. Retrieved August 20, 2007, from http://www.manhattan-institute.org/html/jpr-98–2.htm. Bridges, L. J., & Moore, K. A. (2002). *Religious involvement and children's well-being: What research tells us (and what it doesn't).* Washington, DC: Child Trends. Smith, C. (2003). Theorizing religious effects among American adolescents. *Journal for the Scientific Study of Religion, 42*(1), 17–30.

4. Wilson, M. (2005). *Adolescent heart and soul: Achieving spiritual competence in youth-serving agencies.* Burlington, VT: New England Network for Child, Youth and Family Services.

5. Nicholson, K. (2005). *Integrating spirituality with youth work.* [Workshop presentation]. Tulsa: University of Oklahoma National Resource Center for Youth Services.

MELANIE WILSON *is the director of research at New England Network for Child, Youth and Family Services in Burlington, Vermont.*

KRISTAL S. NICHOLSON *is a program development specialist with the University of Oklahoma National Resource Center for Youth Services.*

The opportunity to create whole adolescents, and whole adults, by integrating spiritual development into human development is enormous.

14

Spiritual development in adolescence: Toward enriching theories, research, and professional practice

Anne C. Petersen

A COMPELLING CASE was made in the opening article of this volume that spiritual development is a missing priority in youth development and that theory, research, and practice would be enhanced and enriched if the field purposefully incorporated spiritual development. Spiritual development has not been entirely missing, as some of the subsequent articles note, though it has been deliberately missing from practice because of the perhaps misguided conflation of spirituality with religion. But once minds are open to spirituality as a topic, its absence seems odd.

It surprised me to concur with the argument of this volume. Why? I have not done research or even written about spiritual development, though I am considered an expert on adolescent development. In my research, I have included questions about religious affiliation but have not considered it enough to even formulate hypotheses about that variable, despite having some significant effects in my analyses. I have not included it as a relevant domain of research on adolescence (for example, see my review of research

NEW DIRECTIONS FOR YOUTH DEVELOPMENT, NO. 118, SUMMER 2008 © WILEY PERIODICALS, INC.
Published online in Wiley InterScience (www.interscience.wiley.com) • DOI: 10.1002/yd.266

on adolescent development, the first on this topic).[1] So the absence of spirituality in research on adolescence coincides with my own research experience.

When I reflected on what I might bring to this volume, I realized that the emergence of spirituality now within scholarly work on adolescence parallels my personal journey over the past five years. Although scholars in this field seldom speak personally, I will do so in hope of surfacing some of the issues.

After being raised with deep attachment to religious practice in my mother's church in Minnesota, I went off to college in Chicago. I missed going to church at first. I recall in college searching occasionally for some church experience that satisfied the yearnings for the feelings I had had as a youth, for the liturgy and music, for the intellectual component. I did not find what I wanted, so I began forty years of regular attendance at the church of the Sunday *New York Times*, suspending whatever spiritual development I had achieved at church and at camp, where the emphasis was on Native American spirituality (an emphasis in camping also noted in Henderson and Bialeschki, this volume).

About five years ago, a powerful learning experience through my work helped me see that I had not sufficiently developed spirituality as a life tool. At around the same time, my ordained pastor husband, who had been working as a therapist (pastoral counselor), decided to take a church before he retired; the church he chose, and which chose him, is a wonderful community in all respects and it has changed my negative views of the organized church. I first joined the choir and then joined the church. The speed with which I took these actions surprised my husband, and surprised me as well.

Guided by master teachers, I had the privilege during my decade as lead program executive at the Kellogg Foundation to lead staff in learning how to better achieve the results we sought in philanthropy. The primary personal result was to acquire tools that helped me gain access to and further develop my spiritual life.

The overall approach was brilliant, based on the research and writing of many. The central source was the work of Peter Senge.[2]

The basic model for organizational development is represented by a three-legged stool depicting the tools needed to create the future we want. Aspiration, generative conversation, and understanding complexity serve as the legs supporting organizational learning capacity as the seat. The aspiration leg includes personal mastery and shared vision. The concept of developing myself (personal mastery) was something I had previously regarded as narcissistic, and therefore not to be pursued. Through this work, I learned that personal mastery or self-understanding is essential to the effectiveness of leaders of organizations. Far from being self-indulgent, it is essential for leaders to develop personal mastery to nurture and support, and especially not harm, those they lead and their work. Unfortunately, most leaders have not achieved this capacity.

Our teachers also introduced human dynamics, a framework for understanding variations among people and how our differences can strengthen organizations.[3] Seagal and Horne believe that the three primary human dynamics—mental, emotional, and physical—are fundamental properties of human beings, with optimal functioning derived from strength in all three. Furthermore, they posit that the most advanced development is transpersonal, grounded in the development of all three and turned outward to community, with emphasis on vision, compassion, inclusiveness, and qualitative group life.

Over the past decade, I have also had much more intense engagement with other cultures. What is immediately striking, especially in Africa, is the deep spirituality of people. Their spirituality is embedded in the traditional culture and draws from their ancestors. Africans continue to use music, drumming, and dance, for example, drawn from their culture and traditions, as do many Asian cultures and Native American tribes. Some songs and dances connect to the spirit world, and many are explicitly spiritual.[4] And they likely engage what Luhrmann calls *metakinesis*, the way emotional experience is carried within the body.[5]

Anthropological scholars a century ago considered the religious expression (like the intellectual capacity) of "primitives" to be childlike and less advanced than that of Europeans. Luhrmann, among others, however, concludes that there are many more similarities than differences.[6] The belief that any group is more advanced in intellectual capacity has now been replaced by more thoughtfulness about evolution and strong evidence about the context-specificity of learning.[7] Traditional cultures are now understood to have much wisdom and capacity than previously thought, and to have spiritual expressions that reflect human qualities seen in us all.

I now believe that spiritual development must be a component of adolescent development and also of human development across the entire life course. An important question from research and practice perspectives is how to build spirituality among adolescents. Considering my own life journey with my relatively recent resumption of spiritual development, it seems clear that it is possible to engage this development as an adult. Perhaps continuous development of my spiritual practices and understandings would have made me even more effective and fulfilled as an adult. Putting this in developmental research terms, what is the nature of spiritual development? While some aspects of development, such as puberty, follow a strict progression within adolescence for all but those with unusual diseases,[8] other constructs, such as identity development,[9] have been much more variable than theory would predict, in both the nature of the path and whether an identity is ever achieved.[10] Spiritual development would seem to be more like identity development than pubertal development. The outcomes of puberty—adult shape and size, together with mature sexual functioning—are necessary for what we understand as healthy adulthood. Is achieving an identity necessary? Is achieving spiritual maturity necessary? What are the losses to a healthy life of not developing in these ways? What gains result from their achievement? Understanding the nature of spiritual development over the life course will be important for creating a strategy for engaging researchers and practitioners in spirituality for adolescents. If these adults have not developed spiritually, and especially if they have explicitly rejected doing so, they may not embrace proposals to integrate spiritual development within adolescent development. Similarly, parents of adolescents will need to be engaged with these issues. Our own understanding of the necessary paths and practices of spirituality is important to the success of promoting it for adolescents.

Many articles in this volume (for example, the first two articles and the later one by Elisabeth M. Kimball) mention another possible impediment to integrating spirituality within youth development programs: the U.S. constitutional separation of church and state. Perhaps an emphasis on youth spirituality could move beyond this as an impediment and emphasize the context of spiritual and religious tolerance.

Furthermore, the link between spiritual development and religious practice must be addressed. In the cultures I have learned about, spiritual beliefs are linked to practice, often institutionalized through organized religion. Beliefs likely provide the vision, the focus of spirituality. What are the associated practices that aid the expression of beliefs? Are these specific to beliefs? Many spiritual life-enhancing practices are promoted that are not linked to a set of beliefs. For example, yoga and meditation may be linked with the practice of Buddhism, but they are also engaged, especially in the United States, outside this religion. Research is beginning to identify the health and neurological effects of some of these practices.[11] Prayer shares some attributes similar to those of meditation. Are both spiritual practices? Are both the means and ends important? Which aspects are necessary for achieving spiritual maturity?

Increased clarity of thinking about spiritual development seems especially important when working with adolescents. Young people have many beliefs and are working on many identity issues (both self-identity and group identities) at this age.[12] Most young people do consider the questions that are part of spiritual development.[13] In the first nationally representative longitudinal study of adolescent religiosity, Pearce finds very high and largely stable levels of spirituality and religiosity over the course of adolescence.[14] Initial family support with continuing institutional or social support seems most predictive of engaging continued spiritual and religious beliefs and practice.

Why now?

My recent small and nonsystematic sampling of opinion about spirituality, largely from distinguished scholars, yielded most of the negative sentiments Benson and Roehlkepartain described in the opening article: "strong reactions," allusion to the "rigidity of religion," something discarded long ago. My own journey with spirituality, beginning steps and then suspension, seemed typical of my small sample. On reflection, I wondered why highly educated people seem to have eschewed this important aspect of self-development. Considering the review of literature given in the opening article, why the neglect of the topic among scholars? More broadly, what has shaped the historical trajectory of spiritual development as a practice?

A needed addition to the study of spiritual development will be a consideration of the latter question. The golden era of scientific inquiry into these ideas was the late nineteenth and early twentieth centuries, and then it declined dramatically. Benson and Roehlkepartain note social scientists' discomfort with religion as a force in society and in their own lives, and the lack of research on spiritual development of children and adolescents.

Surely communism, with its Marxian perspective of religion as the opium of the people, played a role through the twentieth century. The psychoanalytical thinking of Freud,[15] and the entire intellectual movement that followed, likely contributed to repudiation of religion and spiritual life among some. What shaped beliefs, at least of academics and the intelligentsia? How did it influence citizens in various countries? As Luhrmann notes,[16] the increase in evangelical Christianity in the United States in the late twentieth century may be related to two co-occurring trends: (1) the rise in television and modern media, fundamentally altering the conditions of our perception, and (2) the attenuation of social relationships in the United States.[17] Perhaps another explanation over the longer term in Europe and North America is the prevalence among scientists of positivistic perspectives on reality, often relying on scientific explanations. The late astronomer Carl Sagan spoke eloquently on this issue—that people in the United States were embracing strong beliefs in pseudoscience or phenomena with no scientific basis.[18] But these are all speculations. This powerful historical trend deserves scholarly scrutiny.

Definitions of spiritual development

The work on organizational development mentioned earlier assumes that organizations must attend to this aspect of people, which Benson and Roehlkepartain write as involving in part the dynamic interplay of three dimensions: awareness or awakening, interconnecting and belonging, and a way of living.

Seagal and Horne speak of transpersonal integration of human dynamics as "fundamental, essential, and spiritual."[19] They also provide examples of organizational approaches that explicitly attend to this dimension and how appealing it is to workers. In addressing organizational stewardship, Roberts discusses conscious oversight needed by leaders, with a description of six intelligences: financial, social, noetic, emotional, environmental, and spiritual.[20] Roberts notes that the latter "makes leaders the most uncomfortable," but that it is increasingly mentioned as the aspect of conscious oversight that leaders most want to talk about. She concurs that avoidance of the topic is often due to the misunderstanding that links spiritual intelligence with religion. Her definition of spirituality is that "it is about the space, freedom, and safety to bring our whole beings to work." Without attention to spiritual intelligence, "we become tired, fractured, and dissatisfied. We feel invisible, as if no one sees us."

The article in this volume on contemplative education by Patricia A. Jennings strikes some of the same chords. There she defines contemplative education as "a set of pedagogical practices that have as their aim personal and social transformation through the cultivation of conscious and willful awareness." She emphasizes the importance of training that explicitly cultivates awareness and related volitional modes of attending, thinking, feeling, perceiving, and acting. Luhrmann describes the steps that evangelical Christians use to learn to pray;[21] these steps are strikingly similar to those we learned at the Kellogg Foundation to achieve personal mastery. And all of these practices sound like those described in the recent emphasis on mindfulness for adults.[22] Both Langer and Siegel note, however, that mindful learning should be distinguished from contemplative practices.[23] While reflective mindfulness seems to be similar to the traditional contemplative practices, research is only now beginning to examine the two in a rigorous way.[24] For example, Siegel reviews work suggesting that mindful practices are associated with improved immune, cardiac, psychological, and interpersonal functioning.[25] Perhaps the cautions of scientists about concluding the practices are similar are related to the avoidance of religion. Given that much scientific work is beginning to show the wholeness of human beings—linking emotion with cognition[26] and integrating biological with psychosocial functioning[27]—we may be reaching an integrative understanding of the person.

What is the way forward?

In their article, Karen Pittman, Pamela Garza, Nicole Yohalem, and Stephanie Artman propose the most systematic approach for aiding spiritual development in youth. They argue persuasively that the necessary goals are (1) a clear road map, with destination and path identified; (2) engaged champions to form the core of the effort; and (3) readiness assessments and strategies to succeed. Their proposal to engage frontline youth workers from various sectors—camping, faith-based programs, athletic programs—as key champions seems very important.

At the same time, I urge that strategies also be considered to engage organizational leadership, youth themselves, and parents of youth. Lack of sufficient thinking, and specifically the failure to consider all the key stakeholders and issues, is the major reason systems involved with change efforts fail.[28] Therefore, I would put a systems analysis first, specifically to identify the interests of all key stakeholder groups and to identify how and when to unleash their creativity and engagement. I tend to agree that frontline youth workers should be the focus of engagement, but fear that neglect of other groups, even if only briefly, would generate reactions or resistance that could undo the entire effort.

Pittman, Garza, Yohalem, and Artman continue with specific proposals about how to engage youth workers and some approaches for readiness assessments. The articles in this volume provide examples of existing training approaches for youth workers, such as John A. Emmett's curator and navigational guide approaches and Elisabeth M. Kimball's college-level course for youth workers. My proposal is to devote similar planning on engagement efforts with members of other stakeholder groups. The organizational learning perspectives suggest that the personal mastery of the relevant adults—especially their spiritual development—is an essential component of an effective effort.

Potential sources of effort failure

What must we consider in engaging adolescent spiritual development as scholars, as practitioners, as parents? The resistance that has suppressed the topic for nearly a century will not easily change. The key will be framing engagement of spiritual development in ways that include rather than divide, that engage creativity from various sectors and groups rather than unleash reactions from any. Leaders of various sorts will need to be comfortable with engaging adolescent spiritual development.

Suppose the efforts to integrate spiritual development into youth development were entirely successful. Could there be unintended consequences? Several possibilities come to mind. First, who might be left out? Will this be another way young people can be found lacking? Second, delays in implementation must be considered in advance and expectations managed accordingly. Capacity will have to be built among youth workers, scholars, and parents. Third, it will be important to understand spiritual development. What develops? When? Under what conditions? I am not arguing for delay while this knowledge is developed, but reminding us that what we do not know could undermine our efforts.

Conclusion

On the basis of my own experience, together with research evidence, I conclude that spiritual development in adolescence should be pursued as a focus of research and integrated into practice with youth, with a goal of influencing development over the life course. The benefits have the potential to be highly significant, with few possible negative effects for young people (or adults). Yet the fact that so little research, education and training, and practice have focused on adolescent spiritual development over the past century raises serious questions about likely impediments or resistance to attempting to vigorously implement the proposed integration. I urge engagement of systems thinking to consider these issues.

The opportunity to create whole adolescents and whole adults by integrating spiritual development into human development is enormous and very exciting. As we move ahead, let us observe a portion of the Hippocratic Oath: at least do no harm!

Notes

1. Petersen, A. C. (1988). Adolescent development. *Annual Review of Psychology, 39*, 583–607.

2. For example, Senge, P. M. (1990). *The fifth discipline: The art and practice of the learning organization.* New York: Doubleday; Senge, P. M. (1999). The life cycle of typical change initiatives. In P. M. Senge, A. Kleiner, C. Roberts, R. B. Ross, G. Roth, & B. Smith (Eds.), *The dance of change: The challenges to sustaining momentum in learning organizations* (pp. 545–553). New York: Currency Doubleday; Senge, P. M., Kleiner, A., Roberts, C., Ross, R. B., & Smith, B. J. (1994). *The fifth discipline fieldbook: Strategies and tools for building a learning organization.* New York: Currency Doubleday; Senge, P. M., Kleiner, A., Roberts, C., Ross, R. B., Roth, G., & Smith, B. (Eds.). (1999). *The dance of change: The challenges to sustaining momentum in learning organizations.* New York: Currency Doubleday.

3. Seagal, S., & Horne, D. (1997). *Human dynamics: A new framework for understanding people and realizing the potential in our organizations.* Waltham, MA: Pegasus.

4. See Foltz, T. G. (2006). Drumming and reenchantment: Creating spiritual community. In L. Hume & K. McPhillips (Eds.), *Popular spiritualities: The politics of contemporary enchantment.* London: Ashgate; Stone, N. N. (2005). Hand-drumming to build community: The story of the Whittier Drum Project. In J. Nitzbert (Ed.), *New Directions for Youth Development, 106*, 73–83.

5. Luhrmann, T. M. (2004). Metakinesis: How God becomes intimate in contemporary U.S. Christianity. *American Anthropologist, 106*(3), 518–528.

6. Luhrmann, T. M. (2008). How do you learn that it is God who speaks? In D. Berliner & R. Sarro (Eds.), *Learning religion* (pp. 83–102). London: Berghahn.

7. Greenfield, P. (2005). Culture and learning. In C. Casey & R. B. Edgerton (Eds.), *A companion to psychological anthropology: Modernity and psychocultural change* (pp. 72–89). New York: Blackwell; Rogoff, B. (1990). *Apprenticeship in thinking: Cognitive development in social context.* New York: Oxford University Press.

8. Petersen, A. C., & Taylor, B. C. (1980). The biological approach to adolescence: Biological change and psychological adaptation. In J. Adelson (Ed.), *Handbook of adolescent psychology* (pp. 117–155). Hoboken, NJ: Wiley.

9. See Erikson, E. H. (1968). *Identity: Youth and crisis.* New York: Norton; Waterman, A. S. (1982). Identity development from adolescence to adulthood: An extension of theory and a review of research. *Developmental Psychology, 18*(3), 341–358.

10. Grotevant, H. D. (1987). Toward a process model of identity formation. *Journal of Adolescent Research, 2*(3), 203–222; Harter, S. (1990). *At the threshold: The developing adolescent.* Cambridge, MA: Harvard University Press.

11. See, for example, Ekman, P., Davidson, R. J., Ricard, M., & Wallace, B. A. (2005). Buddhist and psychological perspectives on emotion and well-being. *Current Directions in Psychological Science, 14*, 59–65.

12. Petersen, A. C. (1993). Presidential address: Creating adolescents: The role of context and process in developmental trajectories. *Journal of Research on Adolescence, 3*(1), 1–18; Petersen, A. C., & Leffert, N. (1995). What is special about adolescence? In M. Rutter (Ed.), *Psychosocial disturbances in young people: Challenges for prevention* (pp. 3–36). Cambridge: Cambridge University Press.

13. See, for example, Pearce, L. (2008, Feb. 22). *Meanings and motions: Religiosity in and through adolescence.* Fellow Seminar at the Center for Advanced Study in the Behavioral Sciences, Stanford, CA.

14. Pearce. (2008).

15. Freud, S. (1989). *Civilization and its discontents.* New York: Norton.

16. Luhrmann. (2004).

17. For example, Putnam, R. (2000). *Bowling alone.* New York: Simon & Schuster.

18. Sagan, C. (1996). *The demon-haunted world: Science as a candle in the dark.* New York: Random House.

19. Seagal & Horne. (1997). P. 272.

20. Roberts. (1999).

21. Luhrmann (2008); Luhrmann, T. M. (in press). *The art of hearing God.* New York: Knopf.

22. For example, Langer, E. J. (1997). *The power of mindful learning.* Cambridge, MA: DaCapo; Siegel, D. J. (2007). *The mindful brain: Reflection and attunement in the cultivation of well-being.* New York: Norton; Sternberg, R. J. (2000). Images of mindfulness. *Journal of Social Issues, 56*(1), 11–26.

23. Langer. (1989); Siegel. (2007).

24. See, for example, Davidson, R. J., Jackson, D. C., & Kalin, N. H. (2000). Emotion, plasticity, context, and regulation: Perspectives from affective neuroscience. *Psychological Bulletin, 126*, 890–909; Ekman et al. (2005).

25. Siegel. (2007).

26. For example, Cacioppo, J. T., & Gardner, W. L. (1999). Emotion. *Annual Review of Psychology, 50*, 191–214.

27. Cacioppo, J. T., & Berntson, G. G. (1992). Social psychological contributions to the decade of the brain: The doctrine of multilevel analysis. *American Psychologist, 47*, 1019–1028. Cacioppo, J. T., et al. (Eds). (2002). *Foundations in social neuroscience.* Cambridge, MA: MIT Press.

28. Senge. (1999).

ANNE C. PETERSEN *is deputy director of the Center for Advanced Study in the Behavioral Sciences, and professor of psychology, Stanford University.*

Delve more deeply into spiritual development with these readings.

Resources: Spiritual development—youth development

Compiled by Sandra P. Longfellow

The following resources illuminate the intersection of youth development and spiritual development, with an emphasis on the positive youth development approach. The first section situates child and adolescent spiritual development in historical and anthropological contexts; the second provides reviews of contemporary books; the third points to recently published and forthcoming books; and the final section offers key journals that publish articles about child and adolescent spiritual development.

Context

Geertz, C. (1973). *The interpretation of cultures: Selected essays.* New York: Basic Books.

Whenever we open ourselves to spiritualities other than our own, we encounter the phenomenon of culture. Anthropologist Geertz's classic essays on religion as a cultural system and on ethos, worldview, and the analysis of sacred symbols are important guides to the complexities of meaning making cross-culturally.

Published online in Wiley InterScience (www.interscience.wiley.com) • DOI: 10.1002/yd.267

James, W. (2002). *The varieties of religious experience*. New York: Dover.

A best-seller when it was published in 1902, this volume was ahead of its time in examining the lives of religious exemplars from many cultures and times and in affirming the value of experience as a path to the sacred. It is well worth a reading by practitioners today who work with diverse youth and families.

Contemporary books

Coles, R. (1990). *The spiritual life of children*. Boston: Houghton Mifflin.

Coles describes himself as a fieldworker, learning to talk with children going through their everyday lives amid social and educational difficulty. He reminds the reader of the deep, concentrated listening that is key to entering the realm of young people's spiritual journeys. Using the image of children as pilgrims (an important step toward positive youth development), Coles recounts his conversations with Christian, Muslim, and Jewish children, as well as those whose journeys are secular.

Dowling, E. M., & Scarlett, W. G. (2006). *Encyclopedia of religious and spiritual development*. Thousand Oaks, CA: Sage.

This desktop compendium of information will help youth workers be better informed about the complexity of factors involved in religious and spiritual development and better equipped to respond to the many questions that arise in conversations with young people. With increasing globalization, the young people we work with may represent any of dozens of religious and spiritual traditions, and this book fairly represents a wide range of belief systems, including the major world religions as well as naturalism, Native American spiritualities, Aboriginal spirituality, and psychoanalytic approaches, to name a few. In more than 250 short, readable essays, international scholars explore the people, places, texts, psychological and theological theories, and works of music and art that comprise the fascinating world of global religious and spiritual development. Subjects range from "The Five Pillars of Islam" to the "Gnostic Gospels," "Fasting as a Spiritual Practice," and "Mindfulness." Although the volume is somewhat expensive, it will be of enduring value, and readers can often find used copies.

Hay, D., & Nye, R. (1998; rev. ed. 2006). *The spirit of the child.* New York: HarperCollins.

Hay and Nye's work was carried out at the University of Nottingham with six to eleven year olds in the English Midlands. Religious affiliations were Muslim, Church of England, and Roman Catholic; more than half the children had no religious affiliation. The core construct of children's spirituality that emerged for the researchers they termed *relational consciousness*—a combination of an unusual level of awareness and the children's focus on how they related to things, other people, themselves, and God. This book is a useful reminder that despite the limitations of language and relative lack of experience, children can provide evidence of their own spirituality.

Patel, E. (2007). *Acts of faith: The story of an American Muslim: The struggle for the soul of a generation.* Boston: Beacon Press.

Patel's spiritual autobiography shows the process of spiritual development lived out in the life of a young Muslim man of South Asian heritage living in the United States. For young people and adults alike, telling and retelling our stories, reflecting on the events, feelings, actions that have shaped our souls, is a primary part of developing spiritually. This book can guide youth workers in assisting young people to tell their own stories and in the process come to better know the spiritual currents at work in their own lives.

Smith, C. (2005). *Soul searching: The religious and spiritual lives of American teenagers.* New York: Oxford University Press.

This book reports the results of a nationally representative study of American youth, the National Study of Youth and Religion, that looks at the nature of teenage religion, the extent of young people's spiritual seeking, how religion affects adolescent moral reasoning and risk behaviors, and related topics. A documentary based on the book's findings, *Soul Searching: A Movie About Teenagers and God*, was produced by Revelation Studios in 2007.

Wilson, M. (2004). *A part of you so deep: What vulnerable adolescents have to say about spirituality.* Boxborough, MA: New England Network for Child, Youth and Family Services.

Wilson, M. (2002). *Practice unbound: A study of secular spiritual and religious activities in work with adolescents.* Boxborough, MA: New England Network for Child, Youth and Family Services.

The role of secular spiritual and religious activities in work with young people is beginning to be studied, and Melanie Wilson and colleagues from the New England Network for Child, Youth and Family Services are at the forefront. *A Part of You So Deep* brings the voices of vulnerable young people to the table, responding to questions about their spiritual lives with passion, confusion, disappointment, and yearning. *Practice Unbound* is an earlier study of the therapeutic use of secular spiritual activities. It finds that spiritually oriented practices benefit young people by helping them relax, manage their anger, and think constructively about their lives.

Yust, K. M., Johnson, A. N., Sasso, S. E., & Roehlkepartain, E.C. (2006). *Nurturing child and adolescent spirituality: Perspectives from the world's religious traditions.* Lanham, MD: Rowman & Littlefield.

This book of essays seeks to provide a baseline of knowledge on childhood and adolescent religious spirituality through an international, interfaith discussion among scholars and practitioners from multiple disciplines. Focusing on the wisdom of five major world religions, the authors wrestle with such issues as defining spirituality and negotiating similarities and differences among various perspectives. Rites of passage, rituals and practices to nurture the inner life, connecting the inner life with ethical action, and methods for nurturing spirituality are all thoughtfully examined.

Roehlkepartain, E. C., King, P. E., Wagener, L., & Benson, P. L. (2006). *The handbook of spiritual development in childhood and adolescence.* Thousand Oaks, CA: Sage.

Although there is a worldwide burgeoning of scholarly interest in child and adolescent spiritual development, this area of inquiry lacks a cohesive, established base of foundational theory or research. This ambitious, groundbreaking book brings together leading scholars from multiple disciplines and four continents, engaging scientific research in dialogue with the lived wisdom of practitioners.

Key journals

International Journal for the Psychology of Religion

International Journal of Children's Spirituality

Journal for the Scientific Study of Religion (The Society for the Scientific Study of Religion)

Journal of Religion and Spirituality (Division 36 of the American Psychological Association)

Journal of Youth and Theology (International Association for the Study of Youth Ministry)

Religious Education (the journal of the Religious Education Association)

Review of Religious Research (Religious Research Association)

SANDRA P. LONGFELLOW *manages the Information Resource Center at Search Institute, Minneapolis, Minnesota.*

Index

New Directions for Youth Development

Order Form

SUBSCRIPTIONS AND SINGLE ISSUES

DISCOUNTED BACK ISSUES:

*Use this form to receive **20% off** all back issues of New Directions for Youth Development. All single issues priced at **$23.20** (normally $29.00)*

TITLE	ISSUE NO.	ISBN

***Call 888-378-2537** or see mailing instructions below. When calling, mention the promotional code, JB7ND, to receive your discount.*

*For a complete list of issues, please visit **www.josseybass.com/go/ndyd***

SUBSCRIPTIONS: *(1 year, 4 issues)*

☐ New Order ☐ Renewal

U.S.	☐ Individual: $85	☐ Institutional: $209
Canada/Mexico	☐ Individual: $85	☐ Institutional: $249
All Others	☐ Individual: $109	☐ Institutional: $283

***Call 888-378-2537** or see mailing and pricing instructions below. Online subscriptions are available at www.interscience.wiley.com.*

Copy or detach page and send to:

John Wiley & Sons, Journals Dept, 5th Floor
989 Market Street, San Francisco, CA 94103-1741

Order Form can also be faxed to: 888-481-2665

Issue/Subscription Amount: $ ________

Shipping Amount: $ ________
(for single issues only—subscription prices include shipping)

Total Amount: $ ________

SHIPPING CHARGES:

SURFACE	Domestic	Canadian
First Item	$5.00	$6.00
Each Add'l Item	$3.00	$1.50

(No sales tax for U.S. subscriptions. Canadian residents, add GST for subscription orders. Individual rate subscriptions must be paid by personal check or credit card. Individual rate subscriptions may not be resold as library copies.)

☐ Payment enclosed (U.S. check or money order only. All payments must be in U.S. dollars.)

☐ VISA ☐ MC ☐ Amex # ________________ Exp. Date ________

Card Holder Name ________________ Card Issue # ________

Signature ________________ Day Phone ________

☐ Bill Me (U.S. institutional orders only. Purchase order required.)

Purchase order # ________________

Federal Tax ID13559302 GST 89102 8052

Name ________________

Address ________________

Phone ________________ E-mail ________________

JB7ND

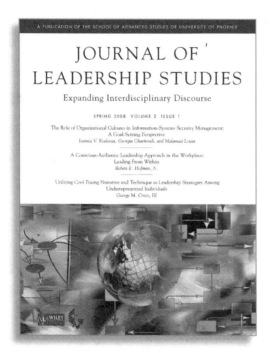